Ecocide

Also by Adam D. Carfagno Cherson

Non-Fiction: Environmental Science, Law, and Policy

- *Towards a New Environmental Tort Damages Regime*
- *Intergenerational Equity and Family Structure: Exploring the Social Impact of Intestate Inheritance Laws in Louisiana and Puerto Rico*
- *Reading From a Vanishing Landscape in Jamaica Bay, New York*
- *An Energy Based System for Appraising the Non-Use Environmental Value of Ecosystems*
- *Marine Debris: A Policy Analysis (co-author)*
- *Eutrophication in the Metropolitan Hudson River Estuary (co-author)*
- *Environmental Ethics From Theory to Praxis*
- *The United States and Biological Diversity*
- *Pro-Environmental Behavior of Public and Private Management Students (co-author)*
- *Structural Adjustment, Deforestation, and Population Growth*
- *The Future Ain't What It Used to Be: Theories of Intergenerational Equity*
- *Economic Growth and Environmental Protection*
- *Rapid Site Selection and Performance Monitoring for Marine Reserves*
- *Addressing Electronic Waste in New York City (co-author)*
- *System for the Capture of Sufficient Atmospheric CO2 by 2100 A.D. so as to Prevent the Risk of Catastrophic Climate Change (patent pending)*

Non-Fiction: Philology

- *Lucubrations From the Labyrinth of Arts and Letters*
- *The Literary Imagination Under Totalitarian Regimes: A Cuban Case Study*

Fiction

- *Where Was He On 9/11? ... and Other Stories (collection)*
- *Smoking Mirror (toon musical)*
- *Everything Means Something (screenplay)*
- *Sherds (collected poems)*
- *Attaboy! (musical comedy pastiche)*
- *Chariots and Horses (opera)*
- *7 Emigrations from Ladino (SATB choral variations)*
- *Splice (screenplay)*

Ecocide

Environmental Doom and Gloom Explained in Everyday Language

Adam D. Carfagno Cherson

Doctor of Jurisprudence
Master of Public Administration

Greencore Books
New York

Ecocide:
Environmental Gloom and Doom Explained in Everyday Language

Front Cover: Photo taken by the author in the Caribbean Sea showing the effects of eutrophication on coastal seabeds. Agricultural runoffs, sewage wastes, overfishing, and ocean warming combine to create ideal conditions for the proliferation of red-brown algae, eventually smothering other bottom dwellers such as sea grasses and corals.

For Julien Owain and Clio Maya

Contents

PREFACE

As an average citizen of the United States of America I am accused in the torrent of global public opinion of a crime comparable to genocide, if not worse. The crime is ecocide: the killing of large quantities of life and natural habitat on Earth. My accusers indict that when the final tally is made, the innocent victims of this crime will be many, many living beings, human as well as a multitude of other creatures from every kingdom of life. My indictment states that the crime will take decades to fully commit and is being perpetrated by a large number of co-conspirators, many of whom are not from the United States. Those persons who live after us and are affected by our actions, if they are able to survive on a much altered Earth, will look upon our involvement in this crime with disgust and horror, much the same way we look upon slavery or genocide.

The evidence for this criminal act is summarized in the concept of the ecological footprint (Table 1). Not to be confused with a carbon footprint, an ecological footprint is a measure of how much biologically productive land and water an individual or group requires to produce all the resources he/they consume and to absorb all the waste he/they generate—using prevailing technology and resource management practices. The biocapacity of an area is a measure of how much can be produced and absorbed in the area available to the person or group. Table 1 shows that I, as a U.S. citizen, need 23.682 global acres to sustain me. Using the national territory allotted to me, I am able to produce/absorb the equivalent of 11.709 acres. I consume 11.973 global acres more than I can produce/absorb. This places me in the third worst position globally, and things would be far worse if I were not fantastically productive relative to other nationalities. What all this means is that I live at the cost of other world regions, or of future generations, or, even more direly, I am using up the Earth at a faster rate than it can be replenished. At this rate, the day will come when the bubble bursts and, suddenly, there will no longer be enough Earth to sustain our current lifestyles. If there is a positive side to all this it is that I need only reduce my consumption by about half (or double my productivity) to reach footprint neutrality, a far smaller percentage change than needed by the other nations shown.

I understand these charges and I plead *no lo contendere*. What is done is done and has been done since the dawn of human history. I just happen to be in one of the first generations facing the charges; I am ready to accept the consequences. In my defense, I have been carefully verifying the details of the claims brought against me, searching for a way out. This book is my attempt to seek out the truth. Are these accusations real? Am I guilty? Is rehabilitation possible?

All Data in Global Acres/Person	Ecological Footprint	Biocapacity	Ecological Deficit	% Reduction For Balance
World	5.532	4.405	(1.127)	20.37%
United Arab Emirates	29.314	2.074	(27.24)	92.92%
Kuwait	18.143	0.797	(17.346)	95.60%
United States of America	23.682	11.709	(11.973)	50.56%
Israel	11.401	0.941	(10.46)	91.75%
United Kingdom	13.818	4.011	(9.807)	70.97%
BeNeLux	12.056	2.343	(9.713)	80.56%
Spain	13.233	4.284	(8.949)	67.63%
Japan	10.752	1.810	(8.942)	83.16%
Switzerland	12.709	3.804	(8.905)	70.07%
Greece	12.357	3.571	(8.786)	71.10%

Table 1:Ecological Footprints (*Data Source: Global Footprint Network, http://www.footprintnetwork.org/index.php,last viewed 8/18/07*)

How has someone like me, the grandson of humble, impoverished refugees fleeing from places of ethnic and religious cleansing and quasi-feudal economic oppression, emerged as such a shamefully villainous and excessive person? If these accusations are true then I can only say that euphoric ignorance is my excuse, and as we know, this is no defense. If indeed there is a way to break out of this alleged ecocidal vortex, it must be through sober and informed action.

I have found the environmental enigma to be a gnarly tangle of interrelated loops, feedbacks, and branches all of which need to be somehow considered as a single whole. This process can often defy simplification, yet with the goal of conveying my findings to non-specialists and non-experts, I have sought to heed Thoreau's exhortation to simplify, simplify, simplify as much as the subject will allow. (If at times my explications still do not seem not simple enough, I welcome questions directly.) For the sake of prosaic organization and simplicity I have chosen to unravel this unwieldy knot into two primary end points stemming from six primary causes as illustrated here:

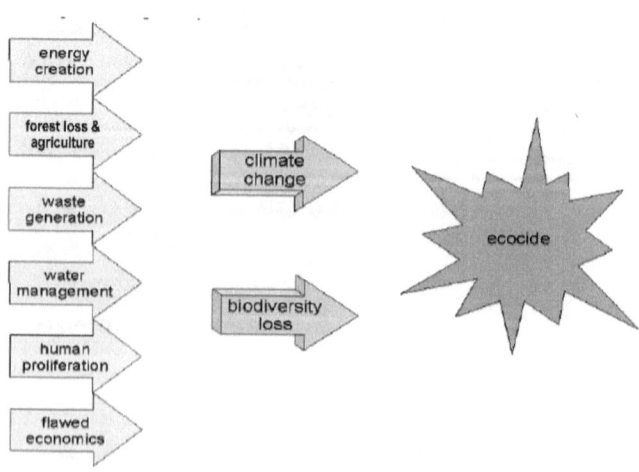

The first section of the book presents the current state of biodiversity loss and climate change knowledge along with a brief but essential discussion of environmental ethics. The second part of the book draws on the latest research and theory to arrive at prescriptions for taming the six environmental demons represented by these causes. My aim has been to write a guide for the environmentally perplexed, myself included, and to refrain from overly technical talk. A plainer language approach will, I hope, bolster public awareness of what the experts are talking about, encouraging a common understanding and common goals. For reasons that will become evident, leaving environmental problems to the experts or to the free business market is not an effective option. The task is so large that we must all work together to effect the necessary changes, if, of course, one agrees that there is a problem to be addressed and that we humans can actually do something to fix that problem.

INTRODUCTION: READING THE LANDSCAPE

Being something of an environmental skeptic, I have spent considerable time seeking evidence so as to judge for myself how things are going out there in the natural world, far from the abstractions of academic journals and treatises. I've joined marine biologists in coral reef areas from Australia and Indonesia to the Gulf of California. I've sat in Caribbean rainforests studying endangered parrots with ornithologists. I've even lived in the thick of the Appalachian forest during my Walden period. Some of these experiences were tied to graduate work in environmental science and policy, others were motivated simply by an inexhaustible curiosity regarding the state of the natural world and my place in that world. In each of these distant locales I have found not only spiritual rejuvenation, but also substantial reason for concern that this source of spiritual sustenance may not be available to future generations.

Like most people, though I am especially interested in the state of health of my own backyard. Here in New York City, we don't have too much wildlife so the little we do have is extremely precious. With these thoughts in mind, in April, 2005, I decided to take a walk along a salt marsh in the Jamaica Bay Wildlife Refuge located in the heart of Queens, New York. I didn't just want to have a nice stroll. I wanted to make observations and to have those observations mean something. Apparently I have not been alone in this urge towards personal verification and citizen science. There are now several wonderful ways for citizens to participate in real environmental research by making and recording local data observations and then uploading them to web sites.[1] Whether or not one chooses to participate in such a project, global change observations are available to just about anyone anywhere; sometimes what our own eyes and ears tell us can provide important empirical support for what the scientists are saying.

The Jamaica Bay Wildlife Refuge (JB) is a 9,155-acre estuarial wetland area within the limits of New York City. As an ecological landscape, the Bay can be divided into natural patches of salt marsh, upland fields, upland woods, fresh ponds, brackish ponds, open expanses of bay, islands, and a built environment of bay side residential communities, bridges, marinas, roads, playing fields, bulkheads, waste treatment plants, sewage and storm outfalls, and an International Airport (JFK). The recent US Supreme Court definitions notwithstanding, for scientists a wetland is an area of land that water flows over, or forms ponds in, or even just saturates the soil with moisture during some portion of the year.[2] Although about 60% of the JB wetlands have been lost since 1924, what remains continues to serve as an important yet dwindling wildlife refuge.[3] For about six to ten years, the conservation community has been aware of accelerating losses of salt marsh in JB. Projections based on current trends indicate that, by 2025, all of the remaining salt marsh will have disappeared. Since my goal was to observe as much as possible and to then match these observations with published studies that have tackled the subject of JB's deteriorating salt marshes, I chose an area adjacent to an established visitors' path on a marsh island smack in the middle of the Bay. The map (Image 1) shows my trajectory as well as the vantage point of several digital images (printed following this chapter). This map also displays the remote sensing data which has been used to measure the marsh losses.[4] Remote sensing involves the use of research satellites to gather geological information from afar. As I began my walk at point A, I had in mind my conversations with Ellen Kracauer Hartig, a climate research scientist, whose paper on the human and climate change impacts on these marshes had alerted the world to their accelerating disappearance.[5] The simple explanation for this phenomenon is that the rate of marsh accretion is less than the rate of water level rise. In other words, there is a kind of race taking place between the height of the marsh and the height of the water surrounding the marsh. Water levels all over the world have been rising ever so slightly over the past few decades as a result of global warming, which not only melts ice and snow and increases the amount

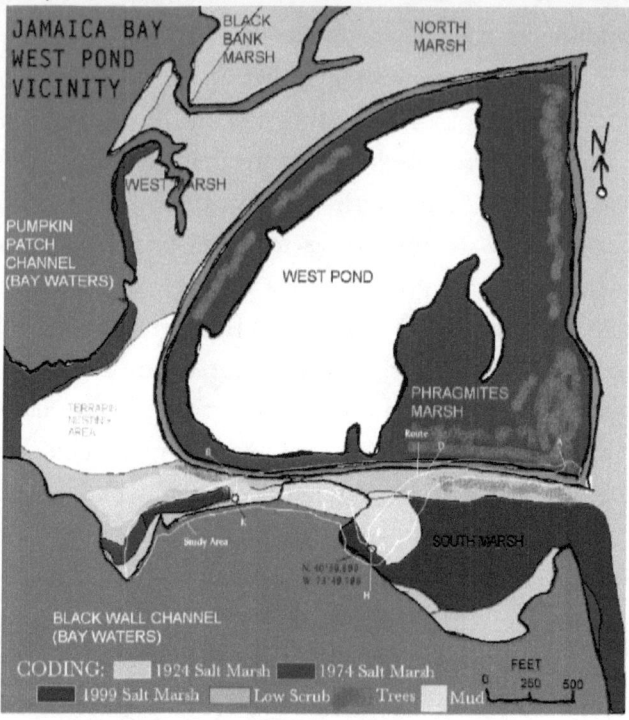

Figure 1: Jamaica Bay West Pond Vicinity (full color image is available at http://image.xyvy.info/map.jpg)

of liquid water in the Earth system, but also expands the volume of the water already there.

Yet not all marshes have been fading. Some are able to keep up with the rising waters by means of accretion. Accretion occurs when tidal waters bring in layers of sediment over a marsh which builds up over time. The sediment is held in place by existing flora and fauna and the marsh height grows. Without flora and fauna, accretion does not occur. The limnological community (the people who study lakes, ponds, bays, etc.) has taken the position that JB marshes are vanishing because human disturbances have: 1) diminished the amount of tidal sediment which is reaching the marshes and 2) altered the floral and faunal composition on the marshes (leading to diminishing sediment retention and erosion). These suppositions have been far from confirmed by rigorous scientific study; they are hypothetical. But conservation ecology has reached a kind of crisis-fork in the road: one must either investigate, study, and research at greater length, thereby risking potentially catastrophic losses, or take action based on incomplete knowledge. The wisest course is of course to take both roads. And this is what is being done in JB. As the research continues, The Army Corps of Engineers has been spraying dredged material on to the marsh edge at Big Egg Marsh as well as planting plugs' of *Spartina alternifolia*, the marsh cordgrass that binds these marshes together since August 2003. I was aware of the spraying and planting as I stepped onto the squishy ground, and I wondered whether the spraying and planting would have to become a regular, annual activity across the whole JB system. I wondered about how much effort and expense that would entail and whether we would have the requisite determination to keep this going year after year and through economic downturns. I also hoped that there could be a more self-sufficient solution, a solution which addressed the root causes and rebalanced the system once and for all so that it would run without the need for human remediation. As I began, I reminded myself of the rule I once learned in a Biology class, the rule of hierarchical focus which says that one should consider not only the level of ecological organization of the focal object of study (the cordgrass itself), but also one level below (e.g., the smaller organisms creating the context for cordgrass) and one level above (e.g., larger organisms consuming cordgrass). I remembered a Yellowstone case study which found that the absence of wolves had transformed the terrain by allowing more elk to graze more freely and thus prevent young tree shoots from getting off the ground; I wondered if something similar could be happening in the JB area.

Any ecological landscape consists of heterogeneous patches. These are qualitatively different zones where the community of organisms as well as terrains can vary considerably. The first terrain type I encountered from the path was the *Phragmites* marsh. *Phragmites australis*, the common reed, is a tall and invasive plant (Image 2). It grows along roads, streams, ponds, anywhere, and everywhere, preferring moist soils. Although usually preferring fresh water habitats, there is a process by which the common reed can become indifferent to salt and can invade marshes exposed to full strength seawater.[6] Although it is considered a "weed," the common reed has been present on area marshes for 10,000 years, and can serve many important wetland purposes: its dense root systems trap soil and prevent erosion; it is an important habitat for birds, mammals, and amphibians; and a recent study has shown that the zebra mussel (*Geukensia demissa*) will associate as readily with the common reed (perhaps even more readily) as with the more traditional salt marsh cordgrass, *Spartina alternifolia*[7]. Although this has not yet occurred, a full shift from cordgrass to reeds would not necessarily mean the collapse of the marsh. Something called a regime shift could create a different type of marsh, a common reed marsh. Several researchers have posited that in environments where nitrogen input is high (such as in the JB where several large sewage treatment plants have outfalls) it is expected that the common reeds will invade coastward elevations and that the marsh cordgrass will invade shoreward elevations.[8] Then it could happen that the common reeds would simply outcompete the cordgrass for the valuable underlying real estate, if that real estate is still available and hasn't eroded away. My observations indicated that indeed the common reeds were reaching shoreward into the intertidal zone, but also that the cordgrass was simply vanishing along with its growing medium, leaving only a sub-surface of saltwater saturated mud. Furthermore despite some evidence direct competition between common reeds and cordgrass

(Image 3), there was no evidence for a complete regime shift to common reeds in areas where the cordgrass once had been. The weight of the evidence indicated that all types of marsh were being converted into mud flats. This suggested to me that I needed to look beyond excessive nitrogen as the sole explanation for what was happening here.

As I crossed over a band of various forbs, I noticed something strange: many small patches of a cactus species (Point D). These consisted of low growing, concentric patches ranging from about one to four feet in diameter. Cactus on a salt marsh? I could only speculate as to how they had come to be there and how they were able to survive the frigid and salty conditions. I took note of this as both a probable invasive species as well as a possible sign of shifting environmental conditions on the marsh. Looking north, I saw that most of the tallest trees in the middle of the island had died—another sign of landscape transition.

I took a panoramic view of the South Marsh at low tide. What I saw surprised me: I was at the epicenter of the Jamaica Bay Wildlife Reserve, a world renowned birding area, a supposed pristine conservation zone, and what did I see? Trash. Lots of trash (Image 3). The trash surprised me because my readings had suggested that this was a problem that had been dealt with. Not only does the coast guard skim the surface of coastal waters for floating debris, but the NYC Department of Environmental Conservation had also recently installed many trapping devices for floatable debris at storm water outfalls throughout the city. The persistence of floatable trash here indicated that either these systems are failing, and/or New Yorkers are engaging in the "direct deposit" approach far too often. I then began to notice something else in the Southern Marsh: mud flats interspersed with large permanent tidal pools, teeming with algae and *Ulva lactuca* (sea lettuce; Image 5). This reminded me of what I had read:

> ...the observed fragmentation and decreases in vegetation density, enlargement and coalescence of tidal pools, and replacement of low marsh by barren mudflats, suggest that the island wetlands of Jamaica Bay are rapidly becoming waterlogged and are drowning in place.[9] I decided to inspect these areas more closely.

In the large area that was once the South Marsh and that should have been covered with marsh grasses, I saw mostly mud covered with algae and sea lettuce (Points F and G on the map) with only a few sporadic grass-shoots (Image 4). I knew this was not a seasonal occurrence since there were stands of marsh cordgrass visible in other areas (Point K). A substantial amount of large scat, probably from geese, but maybe also from raccoons, was evident. I watched several tidal pools for movement but did not see any whatsoever. There were dense clusters of algae growing in the pools consistent with permanent pooling. Could this proliferation of algae be analogous to the situation on coral reefs, where the disappearance of algae grazing species has allowed algal growth to blanket the corals? I was aware that the composition of fish and bottom dwelling species in the Bay has been shifting in recent times and added this to my list of possible causes.[10]

I decided to take a few routine water readings to see if anything was amiss chemically. I took a water sample from the tidal pool at Point H which I later tested at home using a simple aquarium kit. The sample showed a salinity of about 27.7, lower than seawater yet still quite saline, indicating that as expected this is a marine environment. The pH reading came in at about 8.4 which is on the acidic side of average ocean water but not unusual for this peaty, boggy terrain. Both nitrate and nitrite readings were normal (around 0). The one unusual reading was a Phosphate (PO_4) level of .1 ppm which is anywhere from 10 to 100 times higher than most seawater. Being both a primary plant nutrient and a common oxygen carrier in cleaning agents (our dishwasher detergents are still loaded with PO_4), a higher Phosphorous level indicates that plant fertilizers and detergents may be entering the environment— perhaps through the many storm drains around JB that empty untreated sewage into the Bay after heavy rains, or perhaps due to treated sewage effluents meeting up with stagnating flow patterns caused by dredging for navigation. But wouldn't this rising nutrient level bolster all plants, including the cordgrass? Not necessarily: although these levels would add vigor to any plant, including cordgrass, they could also be altering the competitive hierarchy itself. As has been reported, an increase in nutrient supply can benefit certain marsh plants more than others. For instance, plants that allocate more of their living tissue to leaves as opposed to roots may now come to out-compete species that thrived when the nutrient was rarer and conditions favored stronger root growth.[11] Although I would certainly take note of the unusual Phosphorous levels, I was not yet convinced that this observation fully explained the marsh losses. I continued to look for more clues.

I then approached the lowest inter-tidal area, covered with *Ilyanassa obsolete* (Eastern mud snail), (Image 6). I saw over 200 hundred piling on to a crab carcass, and there were thousands more all around. What role do these snails play in this ecosystem? Could they, or something like them, be grazing upon the cordgrass before they get a chance to grow? I recalled a study that had concluded:

> ...plant biomass and production are largely controlled by grazers and their predators. Periwinkle grazing can convert one of the most productive grasslands in the world into a barren mudflat within 8 months. Marine

predators regulate the abundance of this plant-grazing snail. Thus, top-down control of grazer density is a key regulatory determinant of marsh grass growth. The discovery of this simple trophic cascade [i.e., food chain] implies that over-harvesting of snail predators (e.g., blue crabs [as well as population losses of terrapin turtles]) may be an important factor contributing to the massive die-off (tens of km^2) of salt marshes across the southeastern United States. In addition, our results contribute to a growing body of evidence indicating widespread, predator regulation of marine macrophyte production via trophic cascades (kelps, seagrasses, intertidal algae).[12]

Was there a predator missing here, allowing the snails to proliferate, and interfering with an important regulatory control? And speaking of grazing, what about all of these birds luxuriating about? Could the loss of habitats elsewhere mean that an ever-growing number of migrating birds were checking-in to feed in JB every year? Some geese are known to eat the shoots of marsh cordgrass. Was this another contributing factor to the erosion progression? A few steps further another clue appeared: a verdantly healthy stand of marsh cordgrass joined by bivalves aplenty. I noticed that the edges of stand were collapsing however (Images 7 and 8). There is some confusion among experts as to the real role of the zebra mussel in this landscape. Zebra mussels (*Geukensia demissa*) live in close association with marsh cordgrass, clustering tightly around stems and on top of each other. Their waste materials are believed to provide nutrition to the grasses. Some limnologists believe that an overabundance of zebra mussels can cause additional erosion by preventing efficient water drainage during the ebb tide and leading to waterlogging of the marsh.[13] I saw no evidence of mussel related waterlogging. Others believe that the zebra mussel contributes to strengthening soil structure.[14] The stand seemed healthier than any other that I saw in the study area. A closer look at one of these tufts suggests that the cordgrass-mussel combination is a healthy one. Based on these observations, I concluded that the mussels were victims and not causes of the cordgrass disappearance. There had to be something else curtailing the spread and growth of the cordgrass, allowing the underlying surface to crumble.

Looking northwest from Point B, I noticed that there was a large Terrapin Nesting Area. I considered this for a moment. These terrapins may be playing a role here as well, no? Once again, the research materials added clues. First there was the paper mentioned above which showed that when blue crabs and terrapins are absent from a landscape, grazers such as the Periwinkle can decimate the cordgrass. How was the terrapin population doing, I wondered. Could they be failing to control a population of grazers here? And what about the blue crab population? To my amazement, I discovered that biologists from Hofstra University have been conducting terrapin studies in this very area:

> We studied Diamondback Terrapins, Malaclemys terrapin, at Gateway National Recreation Area, New York... and focused our research on the islands of Jamaica Bay Wildlife Refuge...We estimate that approximately 2053 nests were oviposited on the largest island in the refuge in 1999. In 1998 and 1999, we counted 1319 and 1840 depredated nests, respectively, throughout the refuge. Raccoons were introduced into Jamaica Bay Wildlife Refuge approximately 20 years prior to this study. Raccoons depredated 92.2% of nests monitored on the largest island during the 1999 nesting season. We also found the carcasses of adult female terrapins that apparently were killed by raccoons as they came on land to nest. This terrapin population may be undergoing demographic changes as a result of the introduction of raccoons.[15]

So there it was: an uncontrolled raccoon population has been wreaking havoc on the Jamaica Bay terrapins. This could be the reason for the snail abundance and, consequently, another factor in the cordgrass losses. Why so many raccoons? Most likely it was due to the removal, by humans, of some other predator.

In spite of all of this fine scientific work and our own personal observations, one may well ask why any of this important. What difference does it make whether we have fewer acres of cordgrass along our coasts? In subsequent sections I will be providing scientifically based answers to this question, but for now, I would like to recount the Biblical tale of David and the spider from the books of Samuel. One day, early in his life, David was tending his flock when his mind began to wander. Upon seeing a spider nearby he asked God, why was it necessary to create spiders since they seem to be of so little use to humans. God answered him that the day would arrive when David would be needing the work of this creature. Many years later, as David flees from King Saul's soldiers, he and his followers run into a cave to hide. Saul's soldiers pursue David to the mouth of the cave, but when they arrive there they see that a spider has built a web across the entrance. They take this as evidence that no one has entered the cave and move on, allowing David to survive another day. We can now understand the metaphorical wisdom of this story. Even apparently insignificant parts of nature may one day save us from unknown future threats.

Many environmental observers have trouble with another aspect of the relationship between humans and nature: I'll call this the problem of scale. In the words of a friend, this view goes something like this: in the grand scheme that created the universe as we know it, humans are such a minute component that what we do cannot affect the bigger picture; there are other forces much greater than you and I and we mere mortals cannot change the interplay of these forces. I agree that there is a threshold beyond which any human being or all human beings have no control. The question is: where is that threshold? I can clearly affect the climate in my own home this afternoon (air conditioning, heating, etc.). And we can also do so in our cities every summer (i.e., heat island effect which makes built up areas about ten degrees warmer than their suburbs). Just as clearly, we can't affect the 100,000 year Milankovitch cycles (climatic cycles based on planetary orbits) or the billion year lifetime of the sun. I think few would argue that when we still used leaded gasoline in the US the levels of this metal in our bodies and our air and waters were much higher than they are today, or that tuna and cod fisheries worldwide have been in decline due to our over-consumption. My experience, research, and observations suggest that human actions can and do have large scale, short-term effects on the planetary level, especially as our numbers continue to expand and we become a bigger and bigger portion of the whole. Perhaps the arrogance is in thinking that the Earth is so large that there is nothing we humans can do to alter it's basic ecological conditions; perhaps it would be fatalism run amok to think that just because we cannot alter planetary orbits, we should not therefore try keep our homes at a comfortable temperature. The purpose of this book is to show that we humans have the capacity to change how we live so as to keep conditions on Earth comfortable for our species as long as possible.

The key to this quest for environmental comfort is objective observation followed by clarity of reasoning followed by deliberate and unwavering lifestyle choices. Using these tools we can become aware of and react to environmental trends before becoming trapped by them. This walk through Jamaica Bay provides an example of how any one of us can make observations. The next step is to make hypotheses from the observations. A hypothesis is a tentative explanation based on limited observation and subject to further testing, and here are mine:

Hypothesis 1: the loss of cordgrass salt marsh continues to proceed due to the inability of the marsh cordgrass to adapt to changing ecological conditions such as reduced sediment flow and rising water levels;

Hypothesis 2: a feedback loop is occurring whereby declines in marsh cordgrass density and abundance are allowing the underlying surface to erode thereby accelerating the disappearance of cordgrass;

Hypothesis 3: grazing pressures are reducing cordgrass density and abundance while favoring other plant species: a) the raccoon tempered terrapin scarcity is allowing a grazing snail proliferation, b) the regional loss of migratory bird habitat is forcing more birds to forage at JB, and c) changes in aquatic species composition may be removing algae grazers from the Bay;

Hypothesis 4: excessive nutrient loading, in particular Phosphate, from three New York City sewage treatment plants plus many storm water overflow outfalls (and also possibly atmospheric deposition from the air) is changing the competitive hierarchy of the plant species on the marsh, allowing algae and the common reed to thrive at the expense of the marsh cordgrass.

While I do not discount the importance of decreased sediment loading to these marsh lands, my walk through the terrain suggested to me that there exists a combination of reasons why the pace of marsh depletion has been increasing since 1974.

This combination of causal elements fits perfectly into the concept of ecocide as illustrated by the Preface flow chart (p. 9): energy creation and forest losses (leading human contributors to climate change), waste generation (Phosphorous), water management (combined storm-sewer overflows, reduced sediment), human proliferation (build-up of areas around Bay), and flawed economics (underestimation of the need to take remedial action on the underlying factors causing the decline), leading to biodiversity losses (alteration by humans of predator controls, allowing raccoons, snails, and algae to proliferate), and climate change (rising sea levels around marshes), altogether combining to destroy, piece by piece, the Earth's capacity to provide future sustenance to our human mode of existence. Such evidence of global change is being written in the sand and the marshes and forests and reefs in every corner of the globe—there for everyone to read. I returned to the denatured reality of urban New York City a little dispirited, having just witnessed another episode of gang warfare against a helpless fragment of natural terrain, but resolved to rise to the challenge.

CHAPTER PHOTO IMAGES

Figure 2 : Phragmites already in the intertidal zone. Note the absence of vegetation in the lower intertidal zone. This is a strip of muddy sand between the *Phragmites* and *Spartina*. Note the plastic debris. Image taken at Point C. (full color image is available at http://image.xyvy.info/image2.jpg)

Figure 3 : Southern Marsh looking south. Besides the large and numerous debris items, there were patches of thatch interspersed with cordgrass, expanses of mud, and large tidal pools. Taken looking southward from Point E. (full color image is available at http://image.xyvy.info/image3.jpg

Figure 4 : Algae covering mud flats in Southern Marsh. Notice that the algae blankets grass thatch mounds. The grass thatch could belong to the common reed. Taken at Point G. (full color image is available at http://image.xyvy.info/image4.jpg)

Figure 5 : A large tidal pool on lower Southern Marsh (length about 22ft, depth about 1.5ft). Algal growth is profuse. Thatch around borders indicates that grass grew around this pool last year. The grass thatch could belong to the common reed. Taken at Point H. (full color image is available at http://image.xyvy.info/image5.jpg)

Figure 6 : The small round objects in the moist regions of this intertidal zone are *Ilyanassa obsolete* (Eastern Mud Snails). There are literally thousands eating anything they can find. Taken at Point I, looking west. (full color image is available at http://image.xyvy.info/image6.jpg)

Figure 7 : Zebra mussels and cordgrass joining forces. Note that mussels seem to grow only where there is cordgrass and that substrate is washing away where cordgrass is absent. Taken at Point K. (full color image is available at http://image.xyvy.info/image7.jpg)

Figure 8 : Looking west along edge of Southern Marsh from Point J, a nice stand of cordgrass. Sea Lettuce can be seen in the lower right, a goose wanders above. Notice that there is a band of barren intertidal ground between these marshes and the terrestrial vegetation above. (full color image is available at http://image.xyvy.info/image8.jpg)

SMASH UPS

BIODIVERSITY LOSS

Of the various aspects of the environmental enigma, biodiversity loss is foundational. As I write these lines there are various international projects dedicated to cataloguing and preserving global biodiversity before it becomes too late.[16] These Noah's Ark inspired projects are being sponsored by the national science agencies of technologically advanced states, indicating their importance. All of which is not to say that the biodiversity agenda gets prioritized public attention or funding. In terms of theoretical importance, though, biodiversity loss is the ultimate threat posed by every environmental harm discussed in this book, including climate change. Still, not everyone appreciates the scope of the problem.

My encounter with biodiversity loss began with childhood trips to natural history museums that had made me aware of the disappearance of animals like the wooly mammoth and the dodo bird, but I considered these disappearances rare, ancient, and accidental. So it was quite by chance that a course requirement in college brought me into a class taught by Edward O. Wilson. Most of us now recognize Wilson as the heralded figurehead of mass extinction warnings, but at the time Professor Wilson was a respected biologist with a devotion to ants. I listened as he waxed passionately on what he called the mass extinction, a wholesale destruction of entire types of animals taking place on Earth, and especially in the tropical forests, home to his beloved ants. I wondered whether his discourse on the loss of biodiversity was just another version of the critical polemics so prevalent on campus at the time, an argument against corporate greed, or whether his words went beyond mere academic saber rattling. I became determined to find out.

I soon discovered that biodiversity is a ten dollar word whose 99 cent version is variety, often referred to as the spice of life. Anyone who has enjoyed a zoo, an aquarium, or an arboretum can attest to the sheer esthetic pleasure of seeing the remarkable plasticity of nature, but how much variety do we need? Would 100 different types of beetles be enough? 10,000? More? And how would we compare the relative value of the 950th spider versus the 15th frog? Believe it or not, these questions are answered in painstaking, arithmetical detail by conservation biologists, and their work is fascinating. For the average person, though, there are two must-know concepts that should shed enough light on the soundness of biodiversity science. First, one must know that variety does not stop with individual types of plants and animals (for purposes of simplicity I am omitting the other kingdoms of life, the bacteria, the fungi, and the archaea from this discussion). In addition to inter-species variety (i.e., a conger eel is not sea squirt), there is also intra-species variety (for the most part, every bottle nose dolphin is different from every other bottle nose dolphin that is living now or that has ever lived). This means that every species is unique and every member of every species is also unique. I say this holds true for *most* types of plants and animals because nature loves exceptions and distinctions and when discussing nature it is almost impossible to claim that anything is always true or false.

This last statement reminds me that I must, at this point, make a brief detour into the subject of the scientific certainty since so many policy discussions about the environment boil down to scientific knowledge. I wish to remind the non-scientifically inclined reader that ignorance is no defense to the crime of ecocide and that if I have forced myself to understand this stuff so can anyone. I recall a sophomoric conversation I had with my neighbor in a college dorm. To provide a little background on him, his father was a sitting Federal Judge and he was in a kind of artsy rebellion phase of his life at the time, as was I. We were talking about scientific facts. Do they exist? Are they provable? The kind of 2 a.m. dialogue one would expect to hear from a couple of space cadets in a college dorm in 1979. My friend suddenly stated that not even the so called fact that the Sun rises in the east and sets in the west is a fact because we cannot say with absolute certainty that the Sun will take the same course tomorrow that it has taken on every other day in recorded history. I was taken aback by his skepticism. As I thought about his argument, I realized my friend was speaking truthfully. Everything we know and say about science is merely a probability based on how likely to occur is a given prediction.

I cannot at this stage make a greater persuasive argument in support of scientific facts than to invite everyone to expand their awareness of science and mathematics with an honest mind. The more one delves into the numbers, the more one begins to like the odds of the truth of scientific knowledge, especially when compared to the intuitive character of some other forms of understanding such as religion or art. Exceptions, distinctions, and degrees of uncertainty bedevil all of what we call science and yet the probabilities of what is called a generally accepted scientific theory are high enough so that we may pretend that the theory is a fact.[17] General acceptance is not hard to identify. All one need do is search the literature for conflicting opinions and then count the votes, so to speak. The vast majority of physicists, for instance, accept the basic laws of thermodynamics (at least under certain conditions).

Fundamental genetic theory has reached this level of general acceptance and some people, such as James Watson[18], have argued that the discovery of DNA is the single most important human discovery of the last several hundred years (the Augustinian monk, Gregor Mendel, is credited as having fathered the science in the 1860s). Since we are only now beginning to understand the vast complexity of knowledge contained in genetic material there are still plenty of expert disagreements on the finer points of genetic theory. Nevertheless, most geneticists agree that a large chunk of biological knowledge and history is preserved inside the genes of living things, waiting to be translated into a human language. This is one reason behind the urgency of the global inventory projects since once a species is lost, so is another volume of genetic knowledge.

The reader has noticed I have said nothing concerning evolution. While I believe evolution follows from genetic theory as surely as night follows day, one need not accept evolution to accept genetic science. One could just as easily say that the fantastic multiplicity of inter and intra-species variety is the handiwork of an omnipotent creator, and further, that genetic coding is simply the design structure used by this intelligent creator. I, like many scientists, find no conflict whatever between religion and science since I see religion as addressing areas of the human experience which science cannot and never will be able to fathom. By the same token, neither religion nor the absolute certainty of faith has a place in the study of natural laws.

No matter how human beings got here, we are here, and there is no guaranty that we will remain here forever. Take a look at the dinosaurs. Their bones are still awesome in the museum, but not one of them is still running around (*except* perhaps for their distant descendants the birds). Paleobiologists (biologists that study the way life used to be) say that a large number of the species that ever lived on Earth are now extinct.[19] The fossil record reveals that there have been at least five mass extinctions where many creatures great and small suddenly stopped appearing on Earth.[20] As many as 90% of living species disappeared some 250 million years ago.[21] There are various explanations for these events, asteroids, volcanoes, disease, climate change, plate tectonics; the explanation for our current mass extinction is that we, you and me, and all the other humans that have lived here are triggering the sixth extinction.[22] At the other end of the spectrum, some species have been around, more or less in their present forms, for an astonishing number of years: the sharks for 450 million[23], turtles for 200 million[24], and dragonflies for 320 million.[25] Creatures resembling our species have been around for a mere two million years.[26] Speaking genocentrically (from the perspective of the human genome), I want a gimlet-eyed view of the life cycles of different species since there exists the definite possibility of complete and final exits lurking around the history of this planet.

Returning to biodiversity then, it turns out that variety of one sort or another greatly increases the chances of success in many facets of life. This operational principle is in action everyday in the financial markets. The first word from gurus of financial advice is: diversify. When conditions are random and unpredictable (which is pretty much always), one is well advised not to place all one's eggs in the same basket. A drought in the Midwest could send the price of corn sky high, sending shock waves through the entire food economy and beyond. This is precisely the same logic that applies to biodiversity. Supposing, for example, that a highly infectious, killer virus was to surface in a place where all people shared exactly the same genes. All these people, if infected, would perish. If however, as a result of intra-species variety, some of the individuals turned out not to be susceptible to the virus then probably some of the members of the community survive the outbreak. This hypothetical scenario appears to have been the case in Europe during the times of the Bubonic Plague where certain people were spared from the Black Death due to their unique genotypes.[27]

Variety is protective due to the second must-know concept of biodiversity: the randomness of environmental conditions. Due to the complexity of the universe we cannot predict with any certainty which virus will strike, nor when. Viruses are but one of the many types of environmental factors to consider. There may be droughts, there may be ice ages, and there may be humans. If one understands the randomness and variety principles then the importance of biodiversity becomes evident. The key point about genetic variability and randomness is that we just do not know what hazards lie ahead nor which combination of genes are best equipped to overcome these hazards. What we do know is that hazards will appear and that the more genetic strategies there are to deal with these unforeseeable perils the better.

These basic principles of biodiversity are not as easy to understand as would first appear. Common sense might suggest that big, strong, healthy individuals would stand a better chance against unpredictable hazards. This is not altogether true. Recent research has revealed that certain characteristics that we often think of as disease states or signs of weakness are actually a form of genetic variety that provides the group in which they arise greater resilience against hazards confronting that group.[28] This state of genetic ambiguity is the reason why notions such as eugenics and directed evolution are flawed. Genetic fortitude, and evolution, are arbitrary and non-directional due to the unpredictability of the hazards that may buffet a population. Traits that appear to confer an advantage today may not be advantageous tomorrow.

Most of us have heard by now that the human genome is not much different from a worm's, or put another way, that only a small amount of genetic variability separates the life forms in the animal kingdom. One needs to remember that the animal kingdom, as well as the plants and the fungi, are small, closely related branches on the tree of life, and that prokaryotes (bacteria and archaea) and other eukaryotes vastly differ from and outnumber animals, plants and fungi. So when we speak about biodiversity loss we are really speaking about the loss of our related branches; should all the animals, plants and fungi on earth disappear, there would still remain plenty of biodiversity. The reader should be aware that all future references to 'life' and ecocide on earth signify only the animals, plants, and fungi. Microbiologists are far from understanding how the other kingdoms may be affected by human activities. They may thrive without us. What does this mean in view of the above discussion? Within a certain range or variability, all life on Earth is vulnerable to the same hazards, depending on there being a certain mix of gases in the atmosphere, of compounds in the water, of nutrients in the soil, or energy from the Sun. If we were to draw a continuous map of all of the creatures on Earth and their ability to withstand a range of ambient temperatures, we might find that some creatures would be able to survive in warmer climates and others in colder and that there exists both a minimum and maximum temperature beyond which no life could survive on Earth. We could draw a similar map for any one of hundreds of environmental factors.

Humans are able to survive a wide range of conditions, such as temperature, due to intelligence and an ability to compensate for environmental fluctuations using technology. This adjustment is not always easy. Our current understanding of human history suggests that it took our ancestors about 50,000 years to adjust to the intemperate conditions of Europe and Asia before migrating en masse to these regions from the Middle East.[29] Nor is the adjustment always successful. Anthropologists believe that the Mayans of Central America simply abandoned their major cities in Guatemala and Honduras for newer areas in the Yucatan due to the inadequacy of farming technologies, and that the people of Easter Island also failed to develop enough of a technological response to their environmental conditions.[30] Other species may have an even harder time adjusting to environmental fluctuations. The classic tale of extinction is that of the dinosaurs, whose limited variability allowed only what we call birds to survive the unknown hazard that befell the Earth about 75 million years ago. Many of the dinosaurs were large, dominant creatures with no known enemies, however only the smallest of these creatures is still around today. Assuming that one is interested in preserving life on Earth, either for human beings or in general, then one should care about maximizing the amount of genetic variety at both the human and the general level.

Genetic research has produced several important findings as to what the diversity maximization principle means in practice. An immense forest consisting of only one type of tree is not as diverse as a smaller forest consisting of many types of trees. An area that is home to several different types of creatures that are closely related (say five types of gulls) is not as diverse as an area that is home to a few distantly related types of creatures (say five different types of birds). Ecologists call this concept phylogenetic diversity and it is key to the development of effective conservation strategies.[31] One must be careful to remember that cultural variety is not necessarily a proxy for genetic variety. Two groups of chimpanzees that use tools differently may nevertheless be similar genetically, as may be two groups of humans who speak different languages or practice different religions.

One of the most intriguing findings of recent genetic research shows that there is more variability among certain groups of people within Africa than there is between the average European and any African. Furthermore, within Europe there is little genetic variability despite the large number of cultures and languages present there.[32] The reason for this is that humans have been living in Africa for far longer than in Europe and thus more and more variety has piled up there over time. These findings suggest that the conventional notion of race is more of a cultural concept than a genetic one.[33] One should therefore not presume that preserving racial purity is advantageous to diversity. The greatest amount of diversity is achieved by a combined strategy of genetic isolation (racial separation) and genetic mixing (inter-racial reproduction). The isolation preserves a pool of genes for later mixing, while the mixing creates new and potentially valuable combinations for facing today's conditions. Diversity means applying as many different viable strategies as possible

Having attained a basic understanding of what biodiversity is and why we may want to protect it, two essential questions arise. What can we, the community of concerned persons, and I, an individual speck, do to protect this valuable resource? There are many levels of communal organization and each one deserves to be considered. Individual actions are discussed in the questions following the chapter. First, there is the international community consisting of the world's nations coming together under the rules of international law. Under this system, there exists the Convention on Biodiversity (CBD), a treaty among many nations that seeks to set a few guidelines that all the member parties must follow.[34] The CBD's strategy is to treat biodiversity as a natural resource much like a mineral or a forest. The treaty is based on the assumption that biodiversity resources have a value akin to human formed intellectual property. Species richness, according to the theory, represents a treasure trove of biomedical, biophysical, and as of yet unknown ideas and materials, waiting to be discovered and multiplied for the overall benefit of humankind.[35] These rights are taken seriously by

CBD countries, as shown by the case of Dr. Marc van Roosmalen who has been sentenced to 16 years in Brazil on charges of biopiracy.[36] Under the CBD, countries in possession of biodiversity resources are given the right to receive economic benefits from the resources while other countries, more equipped to discover, manufacture, and distribute these products must negotiate with the former to arrive at a fair distribution of the benefits. The CBD tends to equate this fair distribution with technology transfer from industrial to resource nations rather than with a mere distribution of profits. The underlying hope is that by giving a value to biointellectual property then people possessing the legal authority to protect and preserve these resources will have an incentive to do so while at the same time those with the technological acumen necessary to utilize the resources will be given controlled access and a share of the rewards. This idea of a property rights based stewardship of natural resources is a fundamental concept in environmental economics and can be seen repeated in fishery and forestry management as well as any other depletable resource modeling. The idea of technology transfer in exchange for access to natural resources is a fundamental yet controversial concept in development economics and is the main reason why the U.S. has never ratified the CBD.

The CBD strategy, at least in regards to property rights, sounds good in theory. In practice the concept has not fared so well. First, the economic wealth expected to be created from biodiversity resources is not quite like finding an oil well or a vein of tantalum. The flow of biointellectual revenues from nutraceuticals and new materials is more unpredictable and unsteady. Moreover, what resources we do choose to exploit can often be guided by cultural, even political, biases. These are features that tend to impede capital investment in biodiversity. Secondly, biointellectual property rights, much like any other natural resource, are susceptible to unethical appropriation and exploitation by local oligarchs as well as by multinational mega-corporations pressured into a short term, profit maximizing mode by their owners. Both of these problems stem from the same basic condition of our modern world, namely, the urgent pressure to achieve economic profits in the short run as measured by year over year growth and profits. As long as the short term remains a priority, treaty documents that attempt to slow down the attainment of near term economic success are likely to be viewed by interested parties as competitive disadvantages to be avoided at all costs. Third, experience has shown that with international environmental conventions, such as the CBD, the devil is in the execution. Without universal adherence and enforcement, the theoretical structure of these documents, however well-meant, falls apart. A good example of this comes from a recent occurrence in the quest for an avian flu vaccine. The government of Indonesia refused for a time to make available some of its collected specimens of the virus because of a well grounded fear that this information would be used by profit motivated mega-corporations to develop a vaccine that would then be sold back to Indonesia at a very high price. The same logic is applicable to all biointellectual property and blocks the constructive application of the CBD.

Another communal approach to biodiversity protection comes from the command and control strategy, mostly applied at the regional, national or local levels. Instead of structuring market conditions so that Adam Smith's invisible hand magically establishes the ideal equilibrium of utilization and conservation, command and control strategies simply declare some, or all, of a natural resource to be off limits to humans. These restricted zones go by a variety of names: preserves, reserves, protected areas, parks, endangered species, fishing quotas, sanctuaries, and many others, each conferring varying levels of protection. The actual degree of legal protection afforded by these restrictions is crucial to the successful achievement of conservation goals, as is the probity of enforcement. Most command and control advocates agree that there is little point in declaring an area as protected unless human extraction and harvesting is completely forbidden.[37] Some recent studies have shown that the simple presence of humans, their lights, smells, and sounds, can affect the hormonal systems of animals.[38] Does this mean zero human presence? Ideally yes, but in practice this is not always possible. In some cases there exists an indigenous population depending on the resources inside the restricted area. In these cases, continued use by the local people must be allowed but only for subsistence needs.

In many cases the best economically viable alternative for biodiversity conservation lies in permitting a human presence in the form of eco-tourism. Well managed eco-tourism provides much needed financial support to the idea of excluding certain resources from industrial exploitation. A few years ago as a graduate student I conducted a scientific survey designed to evaluate the causes of pro-environmental behavior among public and business administration graduate students and found that the number one predictor of an adult commitment to environmental causes was the intensity of childhood contact with the natural world. These impressions are deep and long lasting. The results of this study made me wonder whether boys and girls of the future, living in the middle of one of our growing number of megacities, will have a chance to share in these experiences. Do we run the danger of an urbanized and technological alienation from the natural world leading to a destructive disregard of the world beyond the city? For this and many other reasons, eco-tourism is likely to assume an ever increasing role if the riddle of the environmental enigma is to be solved.

Over the last several years one group of conservation biologists has been busily determining how much territory, both on land and at sea, should be protected, and most importantly, where this territory should be located. Several years ago a group of conservation scientists wrote in the journal *Nature* that about 10% of the Earth's land and coastal areas under well enforced protected status, and at a cost of about $351 billion[39] per year, would go a long way towards preventing the avalanche of species loss that has been otherwise occurring.[40] When looking at large numbers the only way to meaningfully understand them is to compare them with other large numbers. The world's economic output in 2005 was about $61 trillion.[41] If every economy were to contribute a mere .57% (a little more than a half of one percent) of its yearly product to this enterprise, this goal could be achieved.

The question of where to locate these reserves brings us back to where we started, to variety and to randomness. The selection of reserves is based on maximizing the amount of genetic variety in the preserve as well as evaluating the severity of the environmental threats confronting a particular area. As was mentioned earlier, an area with ten different types of closely related monkeys is not as valuable as one whose inhabitants express a greater degree of phylogenetic diversity. The certainty behind these choices is based on probability and mathematical evaluations of diversity, but the logic is the best that we can muster from our present knowledge. Confronting the environmental demons of the 21st century means using the tools available to us today rather than waiting for more perfect knowledge or better devices. As a new set of environmental conditions created by humans begins to engulf the reserve, than its genetic diversity could provide the resiliency needed for the survival of the entire reserve ecosystem.[42]

FREQUENTLY ASKED QUESTIONS

What are the main threats to biodiversity?

Besides the obvious direct taking of living creatures by humans, there are two main threats, loss of habitat and alteration of habitat. The first of these can result from human expansion and exploitation, changes in environmental conditions, or even the loss of creatures that are themselves habitats for other creatures (for example, the pearlfish that lives inside sea cucumbers). Alterations of habitat include shifts in ambient temperature, precipitation levels, wind currents, water currents, light levels, the introduction of invasive species, and also alterations of chemical environments caused by waste or emissions.

Losses and alteration of habitat can cause drastic reductions in the population sizes of species in these areas. When this happens, biologists fear a genetic bottleneck. A genetic bottleneck occurs when a very small number of individuals represents the entire gene pool for a given species or population. The limited gene pool means that all future generations of the species or population will be closely related and therefore not genetically diverse enough to survive random changes in environmental conditions that may arise. Conservation biologists try to avoid genetic bottlenecks by selecting more genetically diverse populations for conservation and also by the captive breeding and introduction of highly diverse individuals into wild populations.

What are the most important actions I can take against biodiversity loss?

Making consumption decisions based on an informed awareness of how what you buy and use affects biodiversity. Do not make the lowest price of a good the top priority in your decision making. This sounds much more complicated than it is and is answered in more detail in subsequent questions. Donate 1% of your income each year to the Global Environmental Facility and earmark your contribution as intended for biodiversity projects. This is the United Nations financial mechanism for biodiversity projects around the world. They publish an annual report showing where and how they have spent their budgetary means.[43] Another option is to select specific species for action by donating to the EDGE organization:

http://www.edgeofexistence.org/species/top_100.asp, last viewed 9/3/07.

How does what I eat affect biodiversity?

The consumption of endangered creatures or their byproducts would obviously put additional pressure on their survival. For some people this could mean resisting the temptation to utilize folk remedies or other traditional products. There are also less obvious effects. One of the commonest forms of habitat loss comes from agricultural expansion into wild habitats. The only way to avoid contributing to both of these effects is to be aware of the endangered status as well as the source of everything we eat. Endangered status is easily determined by visiting the web site for the Convention on Trade in Endangered Species.[44] If you maintain exotic fish or other pets, make sure that what you purchase has been either bred in captivity or captured using approved methods. Learning the source origin of food is easier said than done, but there are movements afoot to increase informational labeling on products so that we can begin to make informed choices. Look for an ever increasing array of web sites such as Scientific Certification Systems[45] or FishWatch[46], or the Rainforest Alliance[47] that provide updated information on specific food products. If you are buying imported foods, be especially aware of countries that are experiencing forest losses as this can be a sign of agricultural over-exploitation; see for example the Mongabay[48] web site. Besides making every effort to learn about the status and origins of the food you eat, encourage your political representatives to legislate for ecological-labeling of all natural products from foods to furniture.[49] The rule of thumb is if you are purchasing anything, that is or was alive, make sure that it was harvested in such a way as to maintain the Earth's biodiversity.

How does what I wear affect biodiversity?

Natural clothing fibers may lead to agricultural expansion into natural habitats. Synthetic fibers can add to the habitat losses by increasing toxic loads when discarded. Some manufacturers such as Patagonia are beginning to accept recycling returns of their synthetic clothing. If you must wear natural fibers, try to be aware of the source origins of natural fibers and select products whose fibers are not from countries that are experiencing low performance results in the area of biodiversity. Look at reports such as the Environmental Sustainability Index[50] and then at the Productive Natural Resources and Biodiversity results for that country. The further these results fall short of the regional or income group averages then the further one can safely presume that there are resource extraction practices taking place there that are having a negative impact on biodiversity. As our societal response to the global environmental crisis becomes more sophisticated, synthetic fiber recycling should become more prevalent and source screening of natural fibers should become less burdensome on the individual consumer.

Does eco- tourism help with biodiversity?

Traveling to natural destinations simply to absorb the scenery is becoming more and more popular, especially as the creatures on view become rarer and rarer. Ecotourism can be a valuable way of infusing money into biodiversity preservation if the funds are plowed back into activities that actually protect a particular area from habitat loss and environmental disruptions. As an eco-tourist it is important to verify whether your payments will flow to the benefit of the natural site. The World Commission on Protected Areas maintains an up to date listing of protected areas around the world. This searchable list will verify whether or not your intended destination is considered to be a protected area as well as its category.[51]

CLIMATE CHANGE

As important as biodiversity loss seems, it is dwarfed, in terms of popular attention and funding, by the specter of climate change.[52] Climate change is often depicted as a direct and costly threat to human health, especially for populations in coastal and tropical zones. Since climate change is a primary cause of global habitat alteration, it can also be viewed as a biodiversity problem. No matter one's focus, climate change is today the juggernaut of environmental concerns. This is partially due to the potentially dramatic and devastating power of climate change. The average person can understand the meaning of biblical flood far better than genetic bottlenecks. The climate change issue concerns one category of air pollutants, the greenhouse gases, whose gradual accumulation is expected to warm the planet with unknown consequences. These pollutants are not the only ones we need to control. A handful of others, including mercury and dioxins, require attention, but since there is a chance of knocking down many of these other air pollutants with the same stone used to resolve greenhouse gas emissions, I will leave them out of the discussion.

There are a few fundamental facts about climate change that every person must know before being able to consider intelligently the arguments being lifted on both sides.[53] First, there is a big difference between climate and weather. Weather, as any weekend sportsperson knows, is difficult to predict. As has been rightly observed, if we cannot tell what the weather will be next weekend, how on Earth are we going to predict the weather ten years from now. Climate on the other hand refers to weather averages. Even though we may not know what the relative humidity will be on March 8, 2018 at Chicago, Illinois, we can predict with a greater degree of certainty the probability that the humidity will be, say, 85% as opposed to 30%. Such a prediction could be based on historical rates of change, or as practiced by climatologists, could be the result of enormously complicated computer simulations. Climate scientists are looking at much larger areas, over longer time frames, and they are always working with probabilities. In a way it is easier to look at the entire Earth and make predictions about climate over time than it is to pinpoint the weather at a given location at a given time. Since these Earth wide predictions cannot tell us what will happen at a given place at given time, many listeners throw up their hands and hope for the best.

Anyone who has been in a greenhouse or even a sunlit room has experienced the greenhouse effect. In these cases, the glass holds in the air that has been warmed up by the Sun and by the warmed up glass. In the case of the Earth, the role of the glass is played by various gases. These include carbon dioxide, methane, water vapor, nitrogen dioxide, and ozone, among others. The concentration of these gases is the equivalent of the insulation factor on the windows. The thicker the glass, or gas blanket, the more heat is retained inside the space. Greenhouse gases are a natural part of the atmosphere and have been for millions of years. The problem is that human activities of the recent 100 to 200 years have been adding to the atmospheric levels of these gases at unprecedented rates.

Perhaps the strongest argument for taking action in anticipation of climate change is the fact that carbon dioxide (CO_2) levels in the atmosphere are at an all time high and getting higher (by all time we are talking in the hundreds of thousands of years).[54] Climatologists are able to measure the percentages of the various gases at different times in history by digging up ice from the poles and then analyzing the air bubbles trapped in this ice. The mere levels of CO_2 are a red flag that certain atmospheric gases are exceeding the ranges that have customarily surrounded us and our ancestors for a good long time. Is this alone cause for concern? I believe that it is. Will this mean that future humans will experience catastrophic, climate induced disasters? Not necessarily.

There is still uncertainty about whether the undeniable increase in greenhouse gases will cause global warming because of the sheer complexity of the Earth's climatological systems. Returning to the greenhouse analogy for a moment, we could discover for instance that the increased heat in the room causes some sort of chemical fogging reaction in the glass that blocks solar energy from entering. There are all kinds of feedback mechanisms that could counterbalance the effects of higher greenhouse levels. Plant activity could gear up, for instance, and control CO_2 levels. We could have enough volcanic activity so that volcanic ash blocks out enough of the Sun's energy to keep things cool. We humans may dump enough particulate pollution in the air to accomplish the same purpose. New CO_2 loving organisms could begin to thrive. On the other side, there could also be positive feedback mechanisms. Maybe soil organisms will not like the new gas mix and thus become less hospitable to green plants. Maybe the rivers will dry up at a faster rate than they are replenished, causing desertification and even faster warming. The global change scientific literature is replete with fascinating evidence both positive and negative of the possible effects that the changes could bring.[55]

These two facts combined, that we are adding larger and larger amounts of greenhouse gases to the atmosphere, and that these gases could reasonably be expected to cause the Earth to warm are enough for me to reach a conclusion. We simply cannot say for sure that what we are putting out into the atmosphere will not cause us grave harm, and even though we cannot predict how the feedback mechanisms will play out, there is ample evidence already that the trend is towards warming and irreversible change.[56] Moreover, the system is too complex and too large to turn on a dime. Whatever we intend to do will take a concerted global effort and a long time to develop.

As of the latest data, there are about 458ppm (parts per million) of CO_2 equivalents (the sum of all the warming gases) floating around the atmosphere.[57] At this level, the Earth's average temperature is expected to rise by two degrees centigrade (about four degrees F) in 100 years.[58] While even this amount warming will cause enormous changes, it is still not a catastrophic severity of warming. The problem is that the amount of CO_2 equivalents continues to rise rapidly and when the levels reach 550 or 600 ppm then the risk of human tragedies will escalate.[59] Since many of these gases persist in the atmosphere for up to 100 years or more, the options are stark. We can try to capture the gases that are already present in the atmosphere or we can reduce our emissions of new ones either by capturing them at the point of release or by finding alternative energies. Or we can try a combination of some or all the above.

Let us presume that the potential risk is grave and that something must be done. Even so, can we do anything to stop this unfortunate turn of events? The problem is one of will not of means. The major impediment to concerted world action centers around the historically based arguments posed among nations. The developing world says to the post-industrial nations that it is only fair that they be permitted to grow their economies by emitting as many greenhouse gases as they want since the developed nations are responsible for much of what is up there already. Using this same argument one might justify slavery even. Since Europe and the Americas generated so much wealth as a result of slavery then the lesser developed nations should therefore have a right to institute a slave economy. There is certainly a logical flaw in these arguments and yet one continues to hear them. A stronger and more reasonable indictment would be that those responsible for putting the largest amounts of greenhouse gases into the atmosphere should bear the brunt of the remedial burden. However, even this argument is complicated by the fact that the rapidly developing nations are also benefiting, via consumption and investments originating in developed nations, and so these benefits to the developing world are also being fueled by prior greenhouse gas emissions.

As was the case with slavery, global economic systems tend to implicate almost everyone, except those directly victimized. Efforts to separate the good actors from the bad on this global stage are often beyond human capabilities and are counter productive. Wherever one sides on these arguments, this debate itself is a distraction from the urgent matter of preventing future aggravation of CO_2 levels. It would be wiser to confront climate change for what it is: a global problem requiring a rapid global solution without an immediate adjudication of prior culpability. The developing world's view, as well as that of environmental skeptics such as Bjorn Lomborg and Michael Crichton, is that we should alleviate suffering today by consuming today in spite of the recognized and increasing scarcity of resources. The only counter to this position is a program of healthier, substitute technologies, developed by necessity in postindustrial nations (consider this the atonement for past behavior), which is then transferred to developing ones in exchange for access to other economic goods. The subject of environmental ethics is more fully discussed in a subsequent chapter.

If we are going to try to curtail emissions of these gases (as of this writing no viable technology exists for capturing what has already been released) the question becomes how to do this. First, how do we allocate, fairly, emission amounts among nations? The formula most often used (including for those nations covered by the Kyoto Protocol, the international treaty for climate change) is for each nation to reduce its own emission levels by 7–8% from 1990 levels.[60] The hope is that a cap on emissions will create enough of an incentive to inspire new economic models of growth and development that will allow the global economy to move ahead beyond 1990 levels.

The real problem is whether these new models will arrive soon enough. Can we possibly reduce our greenhouse emissions in short enough order to turn the ship around while sailing full steam ahead? If so, will we transfer the necessary technological guidance to the developing world so that it may continue to grow cleanly?

The answer to these questions rests chiefly with the urgency with which one views the problem. If the climate change demon is viewed as lurking a century away or more, the argument follows, we can continue to fund research and development and have all kinds of pilot programs that will gradually lead us to some new technologies that we can then gradually transition into over the long term. When viewed in this light, the climate change issue is often transmuted by policy makers into an energy policy or security issue. The scarce resource is no longer the CO_2 processing capacity of the Earth's atmosphere but instead the availability of energy fuels. Many political leaders have chosen to take this approach to climate change, concentrating instead on energy security, despite the enormous risks posed by warming and the fact that most climate scientists tell us we are in a dangerous situation today.[61] The leadership crisis is further illustrated by the fact that U.S. public opinion seems to be saying that we are in a dangerous situation today as well.[62]

The contradiction in the U.S. between public and expert opinion on the one hand and the leadership direction on the other results from the existing structure of a democracy where political leaders must depend on support from the business community to be elected or to remain effective between elections. These political donors in turn exact policies that favor their business operations. So the big car and oil companies obstruct greater fuel efficiency, the coal companies are against cleaner emissions or alternative fuels, the farmers want corn ethanol, and so on. It can become a self-perpetuating vortex. In order to appease people from outside these business groups, elected leaders offer a public policy compromise. By adopting the skeptical environmentalist's position and then diverting a relatively minor amount of funding towards research and development for alternative products and energies, the leadership can give the appearance of progress towards a better environmental future while practicing *laissez faire* economics. The entrenched business interests, meanwhile, continue to pressure the political system so as to prevent any real change from taking place, and the developing nations, observing this inertia, continue to apply old polluting technologies with abandon.

It would be unfair to blame business and political leaders exclusively for this policy contortion. The average consumer is an unknowing participant in this façade as well. Most people generally favor lower energy prices and tend to demand lower prices from their political representatives. Yet most people are oblivious to the meaning of low energy prices and to the fact that these low prices are paid for somewhere else such as by deficit military spending or future environmental clean ups. The average consumer-citizen tends to uphold a system that favors keeping prices artificially low while deferring true economic costs to future generations. As a corporate body, these consumer-citizens are exhibiting live-for-today behavior in spite of their belief in the need for environmental protection. The only counter to such a view is a program of healthier, substitute technologies that succeed in providing an acceptable quality of life today while also preserving options for future generations.

If the scientists are anywhere close to being on target as to the expected rate of global warming, our response is going to require more than a politically expedient level of research and infrastructure funding. The transformation of our economic system from greenhouse gas emitting technologies and industries into something new will require an effort more akin to a Cold War military build up. At present it appears that military defense spending is of such an urgency as to dwarf all other needs. If there is any way of casting a positive light on such huge levels of defense spending it would be that the military has an extensive research and development program and many of the challenges facing the military are environmentally triggered so that we may wind up applying some of their solutions in the civilian sector. That said, it befalls the body politic to insist on policies that view the climate change problem as necessary for our continuing survival to the same degree as military defense and global economic growth. Any policy that takes us away from this perspective, be it non-stop war, or endless research, or anti-scientific traditionalism, or even the developing world's tit-for-tat cynicism, keeps us from resolving these pressing environmental woes in sufficient time. I have enough faith in humanity's will to survive to believe that a safe charting of a future course is not only possible but inevitable. Meanwhile, there are considerable and effective actions that individuals can take to begin to forge a difference.

FREQUENTLY ASKED QUESTIONS

What is a carbon footprint and how can I reduce mine?

Your carbon footprint represents the quantity of carbon released into the atmosphere as a result of your daily life activities. It is one part of the total ecological footprint discussed in the preface. Much of our ecological footprint as U.S. citizens comes from our carbon footprint so it is a wise place to begin to work. The carbon footprint includes not only the electricity, transportation, and agricultural emissions that you yourself produce or are responsible for, but also your share of indirect and communal carbon emissions. It is easy to calculate one's direct footprint by using one of the many online calculators.[63]

A much more difficult task is to allocate communal and indirect emissions such as those produced by your municipality's waste removal vehicles or the street lights in your town. Few of us have the time or the data available to track these sorts of emissions. Finally there are the industrial and commercial emissions that cannot be allocated to individuals but are instead part of the cost of doing business for these concerns. So while it is a good idea to be aware of and to take steps to reduce one's own footprint, this reduction only covers a portion of the total emissions produced by activities in your jurisdiction.

Reducing one's personal footprint can make a difference in the aggregate and should not be belittled. There are countless manuals and guides full of clever strategies too numerous to repeat here, but by far the three single most important choices are electrical generation, home heating/cooling, and transportation. In many areas it is now possible to opt for renewably generated electricity for your home or business. If that is not an option then renewable energy credits are a satisfactory alternative provided that one purchases these from a reliable vendor.[64] By purchasing credits equal to your own electricity consumption you are in effect buying renewable energy that goes into the grid even if your own supplier does not use renewable energy to power your specific account.

Home heating and cooling are for many of us a major electricity draw, in which case the above renewable suggestions apply. If you are using heating oil as a fuel source, make sure that your boiler is burning cleanly and switch to biodiesel if at all possible. For new installations, opt for geothermal heating and cooling systems, passive solar designs, and tankless water heaters. Periodically review the U.S. Federal Government's Energy Savers website for new ideas and products.[65]

If walking, bicycling, public transportation, or carpooling are not options then consider an alternative fuel vehicle. The most practical choices at present are electric hybrids, ethanol or biodiesel. These choices are getting better year by year and should provide options for any budget and style before too long. Whether you are a regular or an occasional driver, flyer, or boater then consider buying energy credits for every mile you travel (see above). This calculation can be obtained at several web sites that also provide purchase information.[66]

What can I do about indirect and community emissions?

This is primarily a political question that requires concerted action. Talk to your representatives about lowering your community's carbon footprint. There are many creative ideas that are being applied to this end and even an organization to help local governments with the details:

www.seattle.gov/climate/govResources.htm.

If you live in a city or town with a Mayor, find out if he, she, or it has signed the U.S. Mayors Climate Protection Agreement (as of this writing 500 had). If not, then urge them to take a look at this option.

What is a fair way of distributing the right to emit carbon among nations?

This crucial policy question poses the dilemma for distributing any limited resource. Should the distribution be based on historical exploitation (favoring those who already use a large amount or those who have never used very much) or on some form of nationally based system (favoring countries with smaller populations) or some form of per capita system (favoring nations with large populations)? And further how should we account for population changes, both natural and due to migration? A fair system would combine these factors in such a way as to remain faithful to the ultimate goal of keeping total emissions at the scientifically determined level. One possible system is illustrated in the following table:

TABLE 2: Simulated Green House Gas (GHG) Reductions by 2050

	GHG 1997	Pop. 1997	Per Capita GHG 1997	World Per Capita GHG 1997	Equality Adjusted 1997 X ¼	Base GHG 1997	2050 GHG (50% Base)	Annual Popul. Grth. (natural only)	Per Cap GHG 2050	GHG Reduc. % (total/per cap)
A	24	9K	.002667	.00106	-4.8085	19.19	10.20	0	.001133	58/57.5
B	24	9K	.002667	.00106	-4.8085	19.19	10.20	.02	.000616	58/76.9
C	15	5K	.003	.00106	-3.2270	11.77	6.29	0	.001258	58/58.1
D	15	15K	.001	.00106	0.3191	15.32	7.62	.001	.000488	49/51.2
E	10	20K	.0005	.00106	3.7589	13.76	6.41	-.001	.000335	36/33.1
F	3	9K	.000333	.00106	2.1915	5.19	2.52	0	.000256	23/22.6
G	3	9K	.000333	.00106	2.1915	5.19	2.52	-.001	.000269	23/19.2
H	3	9K	.000333	.00106	2.1915	5.19	2.52	.001	.000246	23/25.7
I	3	9K	.000333	.00106	2.1915	5.19	2.52	.002	.000238	23/28.6
Ttl	100	80K	.00125				50			

Table 2 : Explanation: Equality Adjusted 1997 is calculated by taking the difference between the 1997 emissions and what the emissions would have been if the country had been emitting at the world per capita average and then multiplying that difference times ¼. Base GHGs 1997 is the actual 1997 emissions minus the Equality Adjusted and becomes the baseline for the 2050 target. For some countries the Base GHG is lower than the actual 1997 emissions, for others it is higher, and for others it is roughly the same. Annual Popul. Grth: Natural Annualized Population Growth (growth only from births to citizens, not from immigration). (larger version of Table 2 is available here: http://image.xyvy.info/Table2.jpg)

Countries such as A and B with large current emissions and mid-sized populations would have to

71

reduce most, but a larger growth rate in B leads to larger per capita reductions. Moderate emitters with large populations and a negative natural growth rate, such as E, would be required to reduce emissions moderately. Countries such as F-I with small current emissions would need to reduce only a small amount but would benefit even more by limiting population growth. This system will encourage all nations to produce renewable and clean energy, requiring high emitters to reduce both total and per capita emissions much more than low scale emitters while providing an incentive to control population growth (I would also recommend not counting population growth from immigration so as to provide an incentive for countries to accept greater numbers of economic and political refugees). Countries able to cut emissions below individual targets would be permitted to sell credits to others under a well regulated system of carbon emissions trading.[67] It should be remembered that this plan is not a reflection of energy use and consumption, only of GHG emissions. A country that is able to shift over to non-emitting forms of energy would be free to use as much as desired.

Should I cook with natural gas or electricity (microwave, toaster, etc.) to lower my carbon footprint?

The answer to this question varies from place to place and is based on the carbon footprint left by the electricity generation in your area. I will use my home in New York City as an example of how to figure this out. I have a gas range that has two burner sizes. The larger is rated at 10,000 BTUs and the smaller at 6,000. These ratings are usually found on the appliance's serial plate or in the manuals. One hour at full throttle produces 10 or 6 thousand BTUs. My microwave is a 1200 watt model. If operated at high power for one hour, the device is going to consume 1.2 KWh of electricity. In New York City, electricity production creates an average of 1,038 pounds of CO_2 per MWh (one megawatt is 1000 kilowatts) or 1.038 pounds per kilowatt-hour.[68] Since 1 BTU of natural gas produces .000117 pounds of CO_2 , 10,000 produces 1.17 pounds, and 6,000, .067.[69] So 1 hour of microwave use at the highest setting and one hour of natural gas stovetop usage (once again at the highest setting) produce 1.246 and 1.17 pounds of CO_2, respectively. In order to compare the carbon footprints of gas versus electric cookery one then takes the cooking times and power levels to arrive at a final comparison.

If I boil a cup of water in the microwave (five minutes at high), I will be adding about .109 pounds of CO_2 to the atmosphere. If I boil the water on the smaller burner on the stove (ten minutes at half throttle) I will have added .033 pounds of CO_2. So from the greenhouse gas emissions perspective it is better to boil water on the stove. I hasten to add that a strict price-cost analysis of this procedure leads to another conclusion. The .105 KWh of electricity consumed by my microwave costs me 2 cents (at .20 cents per KWh) while the ten minutes (500 BTUs) of natural gas combustion costs me 9.5 cents (at .00019 cents per BTU or $19.57 per 1000ft3). I can choose either to pay the extra few cents in order to reduce my carbon footprint or to pay less and pollute more. I choose to pay the extra few cents to lower my footprint. This choice represents in microcosm the choice facing us in many areas of our lives.

What can I say to environmental skeptics who think that world poverty is more important than climate change?

Not to take anything away from Michael Crichton's brilliant flights of the imagination, which we will surely miss, his thoughts regarding the need for action to combat global warming require comment. Mr. Crichton, along with Bjorn Lomborg and many others, have taken the position best left to Lomborg's own words: "...global warming is not anywhere near the most important problem facing the world. What matters is making the developing countries rich and giving citizens of developed countries even greater opportunities."[70] The environmental skeptics take as a starting point that the cost to the world of global warming under a business as usual (do absolutely nothing to curb warming) will be about US$5 Trillion through 2100. Meanwhile they use a figure of about US$107 Trillion as the projected cost of CO_2 reductions to a level recommended by the IPCC. So doing something about global warming results in a net loss to the world's welfare. These figures are in turn based on the work of economists such as William Nordhaus and others whose Integrated Climate-Economy Models attempt to calculate these total costs.

I'm not going to argue the assumptions of the Climate-Economy Models. Herman Daly and other Ecological Economists have taken care of these points (see Flawed Economics). My main point is to rectify a couple of misconceptions about the views of the environmental skeptics. First, it must be pointed out that their attacks are mainly directed towards the policy of full implementation of the IPCC CO_2 reduction plan, either at the global or the regional level (which is even more costly (about \$US140 Trillion). Instead, they suggest that there is a safe and reasonable 'optimal' CO_2 abatement plan which would actually produce a net welfare gain of US\$245 Billion by 2100. Their optimal plan suggests a 7% reduction from 1995 global emissions starting now and expanding to an 11% reduction by 2100.[71]

Second, it must be remembered that the environmental skeptics readily admit that if we were to fully implement the most drastic IPCC reduction measures, at total cost of about 2-4 percent of global GDP per year, then we would only be offsetting, or delaying, the world's economic growth (that would otherwise have been achieved) by only 1 year![72] So really what they are saying is not that full implementation of an IPCC plan would make us go broke — not at all, but that it would delay growth for a short time.

Third, the debate is often posed as a choice between doing something for global warming and doing something for global economic growth. Mr. Crichton was fond of saying that we should be spending money on developing the economies of poor nations than on worrying about climate change. This is a false choice. Says Lomborg: "UNICEF estimates that just $70-80 billion a year could give all Third World inhabitants access to the basics like health, education, water, and sanitation," compared to a projected cost of about $150 billion per year to implement CO_2 reductions.[73] But, and this is the key point: WE CAN AFFORD TO DO BOTH! Here is how the skeptics express this: "...[O]ne could be tempted to suggest that we are actually so rich that we can afford both to pay a partial insurance premium against global warming (at 2-4 percent of GDP) [which is how they describe full IPCC implementation], and to help the developing world (a further 2 percent), because doing so would only offset growth by about 2-3 years. And that is true. I am still not convinced that there is any point in spending 2-4 percent on a pretty insignificant insurance policy, when we and our descendants could benefit far more from the same investment placed elsewhere. But it is correct that we are actually wealthy enough to do so."[74]

Lomborg and the skeptics leave us with an evaluation of the risks posed by CO_2 accumulation. These words, written sometime between 1998 and 2004 were based on the knowledge of global climate change at the time. Since then it appears that the effects of climate change are appearing faster than expected. Furthermore, their analyses stop at 2100. Supposing we project the business as usual approach with regard to CO_2 emissions out to 2200 or 2300. Do the risks remain the same? Is there no limit to how much CO_2 we can pump in to the atmosphere? Why leave for tomorrow what we can do today? Even the skeptics admit that CO_2 accumulation is not fiction. None of us can predict its consequences. Many of us do not wish to take the risk lying down and would be willing to delay global economic growth for 2-3 years to avert the possibility of severe ecocide.

If we were all to agree that starting tomorrow morning something must be done to prevent the risk of catastrophic climate change, what could be done?

The answer to this question could, and has, filled many books. I'm going to give a one page version: 1) implement energy efficiency and consumption reductions full force, 2) implement renewable energy generation full force, and 3) implement atmospheric carbon capture and sequestration full force. The first two (discussed in the Energy section of this book) are often touted as the only means necessary to prevent the risk, but my calculations suggest that these measures will not take effect rapidly enough to bring atmospheric levels of CO_2 back down to a historically normal range within a short enough time. Therefore we must consider the need to capture large quantities of CO_2 from the atmosphere and to store them away for hundreds of years. This is the motivation behind the projects being submitted to Sir Richard Branson's Virgin Earth Challenge and, in a simplified schematic form, here is one such plan that could be put to work:

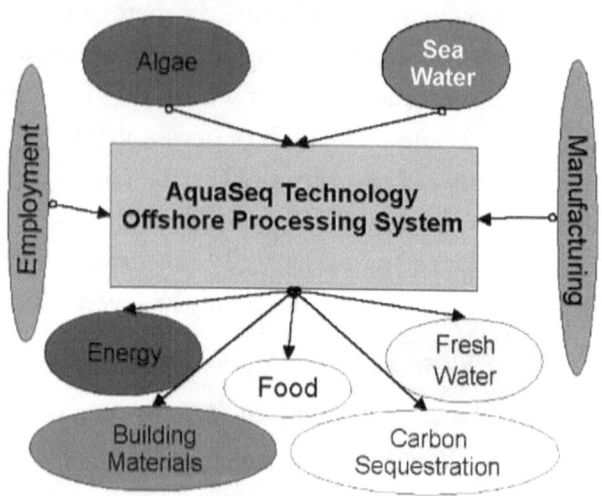

Enough carbon crop could be grown year after year (while also staying clear of interference with food crop production), capturing sufficient quantities of atmospheric CO_2 to make a difference. The growing space required would depend on the growth habits of the crop(s) being used. The most productive species would need about .5% to 2% of the global surface on which to grow. About 16,500 processing plants, each assisted by heavy machinery and transportation services, would be needed to carry out the chemical transformations. Many hundreds of thousands of jobs would be created and the project's duration would depend on the rapidity of implementation of parts 1 and 2, above. Project completion occurs when atmospheric CO_2 levels have been returned to 350ppm and net human emissions have been reduced (by conversion to renewable energies and efficiency) to a level consistent with a stable atmospheric CO_2 concentration of 350ppm. If global CO_2 emissions were to remain, on average, at 2007 levels, then at least 90 years of operation would be needed. This is a huge project of course, but if one considers that there are around 50,000 energy plants around the world and over 8,000 in the US alone, the whole thing starts to appear less insurmountable—and it would make for an enormous economic stimulus package. The industrialization of carbon capture and sequestration is much more than just theoretically possible. I have detailed one such economically feasible proposal, currently being considered for a patent, that will be fully described from the Ecocide website in due time.

I've heard that the amount of Green House Gases humans put into the atmosphere pales in comparison to natural emissions. If this is so, then why do our relatively insignificant emissions matter so much?

Many people look at the amount of human GHG emission compared to that of natural processes such as volcanoes and evaporation (water vapor is also a

GHG), and are amazed to find how little we emit compared to these natural processes (we are responsible for something like 10% of the total amount). How can our little amount make any difference? The reason it can is that the Earth has had millions of years to create and adjust to its atmospheric cycles, while our extra 10% has come pouring in over a period of barely over a century. What we add has a much greater effect on the overall atmospheric levels than the relative emissions percentage implies. Here is another way of looking at it: supposing you have a landscape filled with ponds each with capacity of 10 liters. Natural precipitation fills each pond with a fluctuating amount of water ranging from 7.5 to 9.5 liters. Then someone comes along to add 1 liter of water taken from a huge nearby lake to each 10 liter pond. Now the fluctuating pond range is between 8.5 and 10.5 liters, meaning that sometimes the ponds overflow, bringing their water volume back to 10 liters. A little later someone adds another liter to each pond and this new flooding cycle begins to repeat. Over time, the repeated flooding causes the pond edges to erode, forming larger ponds that are still subjected to the same natural water cycles and human water input of 10 percent of pond capacity. Eventually all the ponds in the area merge to form one large body of water with no dry land in between. The amount added to the ponds is only about 10 percent of the total water input into the pond and yet it is enough to permanently change the entire landscape ecosystem.

TRAGEDIES OF THE COMMONS

By calling this book *Ecocide*, I have intentionally framed the subject matter as a psychological condition. This may seem a strange choice for a subject that is rooted in the hard sciences, but I have come to view the environmental problem as a problem of psychology as much as one of chemistry, biology, or geophysics. How else does one explain profoundly self-destructive behavior? Since I firmly believe that what, or how, we think about the environment precedes our actions towards the environment, then it is germane to begin the process of reconstruction with a brief look at environmental psychology (also called environmental ethics). Throughout the hard science sections that follow I will then be able to associate certain environmental policy positions with the underlying psychological framework presented in this chapter. Environmental ethics is a notoriously dense and dry subject, but its ramifications are absolutely essential to a complete understanding of ecocidal behavior. Although I have made a supreme effort to sugar coat the ethical discussion, readers with limited time may proceed to the next chapter with only minor discontinuity.

Many of us who have been watching the environmental scene are familiar with a fundamental metaphor that has become known as the tragedy of the commons ('TOC'; not as in common folk, but as in common resources like air and water). This phrase, as far as I know, was coined by a biologist named Garret Hardin way back in 1968[75] and depicts, in its classical sense, a quandary of moral reasoning that goes like this:

1) My family is hungry.

2) There are so many fish in the sea.

3) If I take one there will still be plenty left, so

4) My taking will not upset the natural order

This otherwise solid syllogism, which I'll call TOC1, is flawed in one sense: an increase in the number of people and who act according to its conclusion and/or a decrease in the number of fish could render it false. Eventually someone could very well be taking the last fish and there is really no way of knowing who or when that will be. It is a situation where one person's action will probably not have a harmful result, but the cumulative actions of many people could, and indeed will, waste the resource. The syllogism reminds me of the old moral riddle that asks whether a starving person who steals a loaf of bread is committing a crime. In both cases, the actions of individuals whose survival is at stake seems justified, whereas paradoxically if everyone were to behave according to this code we would have the depletion of a valuable resource (fish or social order and public security). The tragedy of the commons applies not only to the consumption of depletable natural resources such as food or energy but also to the consumption of what are called ecosystem services. Ecosystem services consist of a variety of processes performed by nature such as waste disposal, water distribution, nutrient recycling, and carbon cycling, just to name a few.

The tragedy or, if one prefers, the riddle of the commons is the core problem of the environmental enigma and must precede every other discussion of the topic. The solution to the problem, insofar as a solution is attainable, boils down to something economists call equity, intra-generational equity and intergenerational equity. The 99 cent translations of these two kinds of equity are sharing, in which resources are spread to people who need them today, and saving, in which resources are spread to people who will need them in the future. Both sharing and saving seek to reduce the demand pressure on the resource. Most real world conflicts concerning the environment are between people who lean towards one or the other of these poles, sharing or saving. However, I have come to understand that this dichotomy is a canard.

In the trenches of environmentalism one often sees social battles pitting savers against sharers arguing whether a certain resource should or should not be exploited. Should we save a forest or allow local communities to turn those trees into valuable timber? How about this area for gas wells? Or this one, for bio-fuel agriculture? Should we pollute the atmosphere or the waters in order to raise living standards? These are all saving versus sharing arguments. The sharers urge us to use these resources to our benefit now with jobs and profits spreading their blessings throughout the community. The savers say that if we help ourselves today then future generations will not have the same opportunity to benefit. The debate raises a profound philosophical question: is there something inherently superior about the people of the future that makes their needs superior to those who are around today? In the context of our current global economy, should we condemn someone to starve today simply because we do not want some not as yet born person to starve?

Supposing we want to update the classical tragedy of the commons concept to admit our knowledge of scarcity as well as the notion that lives in being are worth as much as future lives. The new syllogism, which I'll call TOC2, goes something like this:

1) My family is hungry.

2) My measurements tell me there aren't many fish left in the sea.

3) If I take one there will be even fewer.

4) But the lives of my dear ones are worth just as much as any future lives (human or otherwise), so

5) My taking is justified.

According to the tragedies of the commons (both TOC1 and TOC2), whether the resource is perceived to be plentiful or scarce, the needy individual seems always justified in taking to survive. This is why many observers believe that immediate, individual use arguments will always prevail over sharing or saving, leaving us little hope for effective long term environmental sustainability. I disagree, for if we are able to shift our world view away from TOC1 and towards TOC2, a new approach towards environmental use will follow that makes irrelevant whether one is a sharer or a saver.

If one believes that TOC1 conditions of abundance apply then there is not much of a reason to worry. One may simply go on consuming mindlessly. For most of human history this has been the generally accepted state of the world. It is the world view that propelled the vast majority of our ancestors and imbues our received traditions (except for temporary anomalies like droughts and pests). For example, when the U.S. Constitution was framed, there was never a thought, to my knowledge, of including an environmental or resources clause protecting the right to a clean and productive environment because these resources were deemed to be virtually inexhaustible. If, on the other hand, one believes in TOC2 conditions of scarcity then one would begin to make choices based on reducing demand or increasing supply that would also seek to maximize the productivity and useful life of the resource, whether or not one is inclined to exploit the resource for those alive today or save it for those yet to be born. Even the immediate, individual use taker who shares only with himself can understand the advantage of prolonging resource availability as long as possible.

What he have constructed so far is a simple four way thought box. On one axis is the perception of scarcity and on the other is the preference for sharing today or sharing with tomorrow (i.e., saving). For the rest of this discussion I will refer to the scarcity poles as TOC1 and 2, and the sharing and saving poles as the carpist and the eutopian. The eutopians are the futurists who tend to believe in the TOC2, or scarcity, view.[76] They are savers who believe that lives not yet in existence are as valuable as present lives and that our actions today can make a difference to non-existent lives tomorrow. The carpists are those that want to seize and share the Earth now for the immediate benefit of those who are alive at this moment. Carpists can just as easily believe in TOC1 or TOC2 scarcity. They are for the here and now either because there is no reason not to be or because present lives are as valuable, if not more so, than future ones.

One could say that eutopians claim as their protectorate one group of weakly represented people, those who are not yet around to fight for their rights. Carpists speak for a different weakly represented group, the impoverished. They value today's lives over those to come. I should emphasize at this point that the eutopian or carpist attitudes do not say anything about the final distributional fairness of any operational schemes designed in accordance with these opposing views. Table 3 presents a simple table to help clarify these relationships. Either the carpists or the eutopians could ultimately wind up distributing

	TOC1 (plenitude)	TOC2 (scarcity)
Eutopian (Future)	Unfettered Exploitation (except for non-scarcity reasons)	Maximize Efficiency (preserve for future wealth)
Carpist (Now)	Unfettered Exploitation	Maximize Efficiency (create more wealth today)

Table 3 : Typical Attiitudes Towards Natural Resource Use: TOC1 = Tragedy of the Commons Type 1; TOC2 = Tragedy of the Commons Type 2; Eutopian & Carpist = see text and endnote 77.

operational gains to the few or the many, to certain impoverished people and not others, to certain future societies and not others, or to those who are already consuming at high levels today. A eutopian policy does not imply any form of economic justice nor does a carpist one. One could just as easily conceive of a eutopian as an elitist oligarch wanting to preserve his or her enormous land holdings under the shield of our environmental future as one could a carpist social democrat wanting to divide all income and services 100% equally across the globe by maximizing economic growth and production.

What is interesting about these relationships is that whether one is a eutopian or a carpist, if one accepts the TOC2 view, it is always in one's interest to maximize efficiency. For the eutopian, efficiency means to deplete as little of the resource now as possible; for the carpist, efficiency means being able to create more wealth with the same amount of resource. What matters most is not the eutopian/carpist distinction, a false dichotomy, but the TOC1 versus TOC2 divide. This is a key finding since it tells us that once we perceive a TOC2 status in nature then we all align ourselves the same way—albeit for different reasons.

Are plenitude and scarcity merely matters of belief and opinion based on personal predilection or faith? My curt answer is no. There are three facts that have led me inescapably to this conclusion. The first is, as any real estate broker will tell you, they're not making any new land (except maybe for a tiny amount of lava flow) and, as any astronomer will tell you, we're not anywhere near being able to migrate to a new Earth like planet. The second is that population growth increases geometrically. For those who are not mathematically inclined this means that population not only grows over time but that it grows at a faster and faster rate. The third is that as economic conditions improve for a growing population, more and more land and resources are needed to support consumption. Now while it is true that the rate at which populations and economies grow may vary based on technological, social, and even random events, the progression or trend is ineluctable. Most of us have heard the calculation that if everyone on Earth were suddenly able to have a U.S. standard of living, we would need 5.3 Earths, at least insofar as we are currently capable of rendering utility from the Earth.[77]

Under these conditions, the global political economy is condemned to a state of never ending strife and war where certain groups defend tenaciously their hard earned consumption habits against other groups who feel desperately that their consumption rights are as meritorious as any other's, unless we begin to take action based on TOC2 thinking. The former not seeming a healthy prospect, the actions available to us are: 1) finding ways of maximizing production efficiencies so that we can reasonably satisfy the needs of people, whether here now or to come, or 2) limiting consumption per se, or 3) limiting consumption by controlling population growth, or, 4) the most likely of all, a combination of these three. A failure in any of the three individual vectors poses a threat to the entire enterprise so each must be viewed as an essential ingredient for success. This is why we should have almost as little sympathy for societies with excessively high population growth rates as for those that consume beyond the Earth's means. Failures of education whether due to lack of funding or drug addiction or fanaticism of any kind (including religious, ideological, and athletic) threaten the collective's ability to recognize and overcome challenges in all three categories. Failures of administration, of corruption, or of political reasoning can each cause immense operational setbacks as well. Recognizing that tax policy can exert a major influence on behavior, a growing number of U.S. economists favor replacing the income tax with a progressive consumption tax that would reward saving instead of spending, dampen consumption instead of income.[78] As shown in a later chapter, there are ways of measuring these three major vectors of efficiency, consumption, and population growth that can help us gauge TOC2 performance levels within any social grouping.

TOC2 type thinking describes the state of the world only in the last hundred or so years, ever since population growth began to take off astronomically and the rise of the industrial revolution. Since we do not appear to be showing any signs of an industrial or population slow down on the global scale, absent some kind of unforeseeable event, human beings will likely be living in TOC2 conditions into the foreseeable future.

Even if we could all agree that ours is a TOC2 world, a final twist to the tragedy makes an effective remedy much more difficult—the 'hockey helmet' paradox as coined by economist Thomas Schelling.[79] Put loosely, the paradox refers to a situation where everyone understands the benefits of preventive action (wearing a helmet, protecting a fishery, reducing CO_2 emissions, etc.), but due to a perceived competitive disadvantage in taking the action, no individual actor chooses to take the action unless everyone else conforms as well. This psychological impasse explains why universal and enforceable international treaties are essential instruments in confronting the various tragedies of the global commons.

Whether or not the reader agrees that we live in a TOC2 world of scarcity, I ask only for an acceptance that we soon will be, or at least that there exists some small amount of likelihood that we will be, combined with a hefty amount of risk. I am not going to argue in favor of a TOC2 world in this book. There are myriad sources for this type of evidence in the environmental literature and I trust that the growing body of evidence of scarcity will eventually convince everyone that this is the new state of being. The focus of this book is on the actions that can and should be taken presuming that the time has come for a major shift in the traditional human paradigm. To those hesitant to migrate away from a TOC1 world: do not be alarmed, old habits die hard and we are looking here at a very old attitudes *vis a vis* natural resources (perhaps as old as humanity itself). Let us consider ourselves pioneers, and our times as the dawn of a new phase of human history that could prove more stable and rewarding than any other.

TRIGGERS

ENERGY CONVERSION: ELECTRICITY

Since energy production is a main source of human-made climate change (the others being deforestation, agriculture, and a variety of industrial emissions), any balanced inquiry into climate change mitigation leads inevitably to the enormously complicated topic of energy production. There are at least nine major modes of energy production: fossil fuels (coal, oil, and gas), nuclear (fission and fusion), hydropower (dams, tidal turbines, and wave generators), wind turbines, solar, geothermal, biomass (including waste to energy), bio-fuels, and hydrogen. Underlying the future of these modalities is the science of energy economics and the role that energy plays in the global economy.

The study of economic statistics is an immensely challenging pursuit. Hordes of economists have looked at and continue to look at ways of explaining economic growth as a function of variables such as education, health care, gender parity, corruption, civil rights, and a host of other factors. With today's computing power, and the online availability of data, this is an exercise open to anyone with a knack for number crunching. After many hours of statistical analysis, I must admit that any patterns that exist among these variables have kept themselves hidden—except for one, the relationship between energy consumption and economic well being. For some reason there is a strong and significant correlation between the amount of energy consumed by a nation and its wealth. Perhaps this is because we tend to measure wealth as a form of energy consumption, who knows. I am nevertheless left with the fact that the ability to employ energy is an essential ingredient in the recipe for human well being. It is clear that the generation and distribution of energy will be one of our most pressing needs long into the future, or at least until we find a way of providing this commodity for free.

Unfortunately, most of the energy we create comes dearly in terms of environmental costs due to our being a fossil fuel based civilization. These fuels tend to be hard to extract, unevenly distributed, and dirty. They are the cause of international wars, domestic injustices, pollution, health hazards, and environmental degradation. Fossil fuel dependence has created a huge infrastructure dedicated to exclusively to these fuels with large proportions of humanity depending upon the fossil fuel *status quo* for a livelihood. On top of all this there are few, if any, viable substitutes available to us today if we are to continue to live fully 'empowered' lives. Our inability to find energy alternatives could cause not only untold human suffering arising from the scarcity of the resources and their uneven distribution, but may in the end alter the very conditions of life on Earth that have been so supportive of human expansion (i.e., cause biodiversity and climate change).

It is therefore not surprising that an enormous amount of research and experimentation is ongoing, trying to illuminate a way out of this maze. The variety of approaches can seem staggering and bewildering for within each of the above ten major areas there are both existing and experimental technologies all being pursued simultaneously. The U.S. Federal Government is studying both nuclear fission and fusion, both bio-fuels and hydrogen, both clean coal and offshore wave generators, just to name a few concurrent projects.[80] Academic researchers and private venture capitalists are flooding the patent office with novel energy processes, gadgets, and inventions in what has become an energy-as-gold rush atmosphere. This multiplicity of new ideas is both a blessing and a curse, for in the proliferation of options there is bound to be a solution, and yet each alternative needs to be developed, perfected and tested before we can even begin to implement the best choice(s). How long will this Herculean task take? Are we using our research and development resources effectively? Where should we focus our efforts? While I do not think anyone can answer these questions with irrefutable certainty, a careful and well informed analysis can help define policy priorities.

To start with allow me to set up some parameters for discussion. First, I will divide the field of energy into two parts: 1) electrical generation, and 2) transportation and home heating. Electrical energy is everything other than powering vehicles or non-electric home heating. In today's world we separate energy into these two distinct types of applications. Our multipurpose energy is usually centrally generated electricity distributed through an intricate grid and generally speaking we use portable energy, some form of oil or gas, for our vehicles and to heat our homes (any form of home heating or cooling that uses electricity falls into the first category). This duality of energy systems whereby some of our power needs are met by central generation and others by our own portable supply of energy storage (i.e., the fuel we have in our gas or oil tanks) may not survive into the future. Many of us believe that the future will bring energy distribution convergence— with all of our power sources and draws plugged into the same single system.[81] Many of us believe the future will also bring energy generation divergence, or a system where power generation occurs not only centrally, in large capacity plants, but also atomistically, at any capacity level (in other words, any point on the grid system can be both a point of consumption and a point of generation).[82] As will be explained below, the better we conceive and execute these visions of distribution convergence and generation divergence, the better able we will be to integrate technical advances and fuel paradigm shifts while keeping the whole system up and running.

There are two main facts to consider about electrical generation at the outset. The first is that almost half of our power consumption is eaten up by the generation and distribution process itself. It takes enormous amounts of energy to make energy and once made, that energy can be lost in many ways—such as to heat in the distribution of electricity in wires. Apart from technological advances in generation, the obvious way of reducing generation and transmission losses is to reduce: a) the effort required to get fuel inputs to a central generating plant, and then b) the losses arising from the transmission of the energy output over long distances.

The second fact is that almost all the forms of generation listed above make electricity the same way, by spinning a turbine. In most cases the turbine is spun by heated steam or gas (both are called thermoelectric generation since they use heated vapors to drive the turbine). Wind and hydropower differ in that they harness natural air and water movements to spin the turbine. Of all the major modes, only one type of solar works differently, solar cell technology. The other type of solar energy, known as concentrated solar, is also a thermoelectric technology that creates steam to spin a turbine. No matter what process, we are still moving magnets around coils in order to produce a flow of electrons that can be mixed and interchanged with any other flow of electrons whatever its source (even solar cell energy output is a flow of electrons so it too can play the same game). The nice thing about the near universality of thermoelectric/turbine generation is that it allows mixing and matching of power plants.

As we develop better and cleaner forms of energy, we can continue to use much of our generating and transmission infrastructure, as well as our appliances and applications. In fact it is quite possible to remake a power plant from one form of water heating technology to another (e.g., shift a coal burning plant to nuclear or to geothermal processes) since the only change is in how the steam is created. An important sidebar to mention in passing is that thermoelectric plants use water for cooling purposes and there are important issues to consider involving the choice of cooling systems and water efficiency that will require some adjustment from mode to mode.[83] Now that I have laid some basic ground rules about a new energy economy, I will proceed to discuss each of the major alternatives with these criteria in mind.

Fossil Fuel Energy

The big three fossil fuels are coal, oil and natural gas. Of these, coal produces the largest quantities of CO_2. Oil is considered to be at or nearing its peak availability with natural gas about 10 to 15 years behind that. Oil and gas also involve considerable political and security considerations. Coal has the most widely distributed reserves and is available in at least 100 countries.[84] For these reasons I am going to speak only of coal for the long term. The following discussion regarding CO_2 capture from coal, however, could and should be applied CO_2 emissions from all of the fossil fuels, although the economies will vary due the weight of emissions from each fuel.

Coal

Coal combustion is considered to be one of the bad guys of energy production. It is true that it produces much more CO_2 than oil or gas and is also the source of other dangerous pollutants. The problem is that coal is plentiful in North America and is therefore our cheapest and most available source of fossil fuel. It is also the default source of energy in many other countries. As strongly as many of us would like to move away from the primacy of coal combustion, the reality is that it is going to play a substantial role in the world's energy future.[85] That said, it is clear that a business as usual approach to coal firing is not an option. The only reasonable solution is to find a way of maximizing efficiency and of capturing or cleaning flue emissions.

These are precisely the goals of the FutureGen Alliance[86], a public-private partnership that is designing and building a commercial scale Integrated Gasification Combined Cycle (IGCC) coal burning power plant with carbon capture and sequestration. This technology promises to get the most out of coal burning by using two turbine cycles, one involving gas and the other steam, while also trapping the outgoing CO_2 before it is released into the atmosphere. Interestingly, the same concept of combined capture generation is also being applied to automobile engines for the same purpose, to harness more of the heat created from combustion. In fact, the efficiency of IGCC is said to be close to 60% or even 85% if the plant is a combined heating and power (CHP) plant.[87] I do not have a figure for this, but an even higher efficiency is possible with a combined heating and cooling plant (CHCP). The gasification part refers to the creation of a syngas (H plus CO) in the first combustion cycle which gas is then reformed into CO_2 and H. Then the H is combusted in the second cycle. By the way, the creation of syngas from the combustion of carbon rich materials provides the initial reactants for a process known as Fischer-Tropsch (FT). FT is a very important energy creating process that turns syngas into hydrocarbon based liquid fuels (refined into any type: diesel, ethanol, methanol, heating oil, petroleum, etc.). As discussed below, the process of turning coal, as well as biomass, into liquid fuels has been proposed as a solution to the entire fuel transportation problem in the U.S. (see Transportation). For electricity generation though, the IGCC plant uses the hydrogen gas component of syngas, burning that gas to spin turbines into electricity. The CO_2 can be retained in the reactors and diverted to containers for sequestration.

Sequestration is obviously key to the success of FutureGen. So far there are two main strategies for sequestration, burial or recycling. Some top notch energy scientists believe that injecting large quantities of CO_2 into the Earth below abyssal ocean depths would be a stable way of locking the CO_2 away forever.[88] This plan is symbolic of a school of environmental thought that believes that large scale geo-engineering of this sort is a practical solution to our problems. The salient flaw in this notion is that the burying operation will be a massive infrastructure project and is in effect a kind of landfilling that derives no use from the waste material. Another type of injection that is already being used involves pressurized injection into tar sands. This process allows greater amounts of oil to be extracted from the sands while trapping CO_2. While this may be a great way of stretching the productivity of an oil field, it does not assure that the CO_2 will stay trapped. At the bottom of the oceans there is enough pressure theoretically to prevent any gas from escaping, but this may not be the case with tar sand sequestration. While both of these burying strategies could work well, they are untested at the scales necessary and remain uncertain.[89]

A far more promising strategy is to use the CO_2 as a raw material for further processing. The concept of turning trash into treasure is a key to resolving not only CO_2 emission problems but many other human waste stream headaches. Due to the uncertainty over whether CO_2 injected underground will stay in place over the long haul, CO_2 reprocessing is to be vigorously encouraged and here are some possible directions this could take:

> *Covalent Organic Frameworks* (pronounced "coffs") and *Metal Organic Frameworks*: developed by chemists at UCLA, these new classes of crystalline materials can capture and store gases such as CO_2, methane and hydrogen very effectively due to their high surface area. Ease of capture, transport and storage of CO_2 will make productive uses more viable and cost effective.[90]

> *Atmospheric Pressure Plasma Processing* (AP Plasma): This process is able to take methane and CO_2 and turn them into methanol (a fuel with many potential uses including refinement into liquid fuels and conversion into feedstock protein meal[91]). While methane can come from many sources, there are believed to be enormously huge deposits

(more than all other fossil fuels combined) in the methyl hydrates located below the seabed.[92]

Green Plant Stimulation: One of the most promising sources of oil for biodiesel and for both livestock and aquacultural feedstocks is algae. Like any other photo-synthesizer, algae sucks up CO_2, and so injecting the trapped CO_2 into controlled algal reactors would create some very valuable products. Similarly, enclosed hydroponics envisions the use of CO_2 to stimulate plant production under controlled conditions.[93]

Splitting CO2: Progress is being made in techniques for splitting CO_2 into CO (Carbon Monoxide) and Oxygen. CO is a valuable compound used in the creation of many chemicals and polymers. It is also an ingredient in the FT process (see above) to produce liquid fuels. These CO_2 to liquid fuels can in turn be used to generate electricity or, if preferred, as a transportation or home heating fuel.[94] The process of sequestering, splitting, and liquifying would in effect recycle the same Carbon over and over again without an atmospheric release of CO_2, provided a carbon-free source of hydrogen for the FT process is also developed (see discussion of hydrogen, below).

There are many promising uses for CO_2 on the horizon and that horizon will keep getting closer as a function of research and development priorities, as well as of a unified and comprehensive energy policy.

Nuclear Energy

Nuclear was once hailed as the energy savior. This was before anyone worried much about disposing of nuclear waste. Today in the U.S. there is a political dis-functionality over the waste storage problem. Every nuclear facility in the U.S. has a contract with the Federal Government that says the Feds will provide the requisite repositories for the spent fuel, for which service each facility has also been paying fees. Despite enormous research and reporting expenditures (over $6B) by the Federal Government, the first repository has yet to receive its first load (the entire record of the Yucca Flats research was recently released).[95] In the meantime the U.S. nuclear plants are, for the most part, storing their waste on-site while the controversy rages on over the Yucca Flats repository (as of this writing, a Federal Court had blocked the proposed use of the site subject to more stringent safety precautions). The fact remains that no one is completely sure how long the storage will stay dry at Yucca, but putting it there sure seems a lot safer that keeping it around the population centers where the plants tend to be located. One interesting counter-proposal is for deep storage on-site, at or near the very plants at which it was produced, and this does seem to have a poetic logic. This proposal is nothing more than an educated thought experiment at this point.[96] In places such as France where as much as 80% of electricity needs are met by nuclear power, the waste is largely buried in one of over one thousand temporary repositories around France or shipped to Siberia or any place else willing to take the hazardous waste. There have been some interesting discussions lately regarding the recycling of nuclear waste which, depending upon the process, could reduce the amount of long-lived wastes anywhere from 40 to 99%[97] (see also the discussion of thorium, next paragraph).

As the pressure builds to reduce greenhouse gas emissions, more and more people seem to be turning to nuclear power as a proven and established solution capable of stepping in to shoulder a heavy electric load today. European use of nuclear power is expanding, albeit moderately, while Asia is currently the center of growth. In the U.S. there are indications of a revival with little concrete action yet. Some suggest that this is the only reasonable way to lower CO_2 emissions in the near term, but one would appear to be merely exchanging one problem for another. In addition to the waste issues, there is also the fact that uranium is a depletable and unevenly distributed resource bringing the same types of insecurities caused by fossil fuels now.

Furthermore, there are serious concerns about the proliferation of nuclear materials being diverted into weapons. There is a heated debate within the nuclear energy community as to whether certain types of reactors and fuel cycles sufficiently palliate the danger of proliferation. Some claim that newer Heavy Water Reactors, that do not require enriched uranium, are proliferation resistant. Others claim that Heavy Water Reactors make the production of weapons grade plutonium more viable. Some recent reports suggest that the reprocessing of spent reactor fuel into plutonium is actually easier to detect than uranium enrichment[98] and there is no empirical evidence of any test explosions using unreprocessed reactor grade plutonium.[99] Nevertheless, the detection of plutonium reprocessing would require a certain amount of transparency and coöperation on the part of the plant operator—the reason that the MIT Interdisciplinary Study considers any process that produces separated plutonium to be a proliferation threat. This would include the typical closed recycling of spent fuel into Mixed Oxide (MOX) fuel using the PUREX process.[100] Other types of reactors using more advanced closed-fuel technologies may someday offer the promise of non-proliferation, but these systems are decades away.[101] Given the possibility of safer, cleaner alternative energies, uranium fueled nuclear power using today's technologies is therefore not a wise policy choice.

Of the advanced closed fuel technologies that could someday meet safety thresholds, the most enticing appears to be the use of thorium as a fuel source in Heavy Water Reactors.[102] Thorium is far more naturally abundant than uranium, produces a fraction of the radioactive waste (the waste that does remain has only a 500 year half life), and is proliferation proof.[103] On top of all this is the surprising fact that the thorium fuel process will also dispose of other nuclear elements added to the reactor (acting as a waste disposal plant for nuclear wastes). Thorium reactors appear to be the least evil of all the nuclear options, conferring also a substantial nuclear waste disposal benefit. Moreover, the U.S. enjoys substantial thorium reserves. If I were energy czar, I would be eager to develop and build a pilot thorium Heavy Water Reactor in the U.S. along the lines of the Accelerator Driven System designed by Nobel laureate Carlos Rubbia, even if only as a reasonable solution to the nuclear waste log jam.[104] As far as I am aware, there is a pre-commercial thorium based reactor development project underway at Moscow's Kurchatov Institute.[105]

So far we have been discussing nuclear fission reactors. Another distant hope for nuclear energy is the fusion process and the International Thermonuclear Experimental Reactor (ITER) project.[106] The participating parties—China, Japan, Russia, Korea, India, the U.S., and the EU—signed the ITER agreement on November 21, 2006. The project will break ground in Cadarache, France, in 2008. At a cost of more than $10 billion, of which the EU provides 45% and other parties share the remainder, the plant should be up and running by 2016. The fusion process produces no waste (the radioactive tritium's half life is about 12 years and produces low energy beta radiation) and uses various isotopes of hydrogen as a fuel source. While the deuterium isotope of hydrogen is easily derived from sea water, the production of the other isotope, tritium, remains one of the primary challenges for the ITER project since it is generally obtained from lithium-6, which in turn is a depletable resource (although ten times as plentiful as uranium) and is also weaponizable. Some fusion advocates are pursuing the notion of harvesting helium-3 from the moon as a safer substitute fuel for deuterium-tritium.[107] Nuclear fusion is therefore rife with proliferation and technical challenges, absent any unexpected breakthroughs brought by the ITER.

Renewable Energy[108]

Hydropower

Potential Supply: 10% (of 2006 levels)109

Hydropower is a multifarious term describing any of a number of methods of converting water movement into power, ranging from very small microdams to the increasingly popular megadams, from riverine systems to the burgeoning field of ocean based hydropower. Although megadam projects continue to be developed in many places, they pose several serious drawbacks that outweigh their benefits. First, they often involve the displacement of large numbers of local people. Second, they disrupt the ecology of the targeted waterway so much so that a swath of species may become threatened as a result. Third, and this is perhaps the worst of the three, damming impedes the flow of organic matter downstream, trapping it in huge reservoirs where decomposition releases large amounts of methane and nitrous oxide. Overall, megadam projects aggravate global warming much more than oil or coal fired plants of the same capacity rating.[110] This trapping effect can also cause erosion in the river's delta area, causing the loss of wetlands and human habitats far from the location of the dam. The suite of megadam problems are so serious that many dams are being decommissioned and removed in favor of other energy sources.[111] Micro-hydropower offers the hope of some limited used of water based power subject to ecological conditions and should continue to be developed.[112]

A far more promising and less counter-productive alternative comes from the use of natural currents and waves using underwater turbines and mechanical wave generators. Some interesting pilot projects are being done with tidal current turbines and this could be a niche source in a few places,[113] but the real power is to be found in large oceanic currents such as the gulf stream and offshore wave action.[114] These power sources are estimated at 350 billions kilowatt hours per year using known technologies, a figure that represents about 10% of the U.S. total for 2006.[115] Being a clean, infinite, and free (save for capital and transmission costs) energy source, this important category should not be overlooked.

A chief liability to the offshore strategy is the cost and inefficiency of piping energy back to shore. The obvious remedy is to use the energy at its source for operations such as desalination, aquaculture, or seabed mining and sequestration depending upon what type of activity makes the most sense for the location in conjunction with the power generation. Offshore facilities need not be fixed in place. For instance floating barge plants that produce desalinated sea water using offshore hydropower could sail into port for delivery and maintenance. Offshore hydrothermal energy makes an interesting choice as a power source for seabed methyl hydrate operations to reform sea bed methane into liquid fuels or hydrogen, or for deuterium from seawater production facilities for use in nuclear heavy water fission reactors or in fusion reactors.

Wind

Wind energy production is currently enjoying the benefits of about twenty years of engineering development. Prices are down, efficiencies are up, and these improvements are leading to expanded use of this energy source throughout the world. In the U.S., the year 2006 saw a 26% increase in wind generated energy.[117] It is estimated that full exploitation of wind power in the U.S. could supply 20% of the national electricity demand.[118] Wind (and solar) have been heralded for so many years that they seem commonplace compared to some of the other options, but they both are potent and simple technologies that must not be ignored. The major impediment to wind energy's take off has not been the technology as much as the variability of the resource. As has been discovered in Texas, the U.S. state with the largest wind production, the unpredictability of wind requires 100% generation redundancy (which in the Texan case has been achieved via gas or coal generators).[119] When the wind runs, consumer demand can be met cheaply and effectively, but when the wind runs out, a back up fossil fuel plant has to step in to fill the void, creating an enormous double capital and operational expenditure. Since hot days usually mean less wind, the alternative resource does little to alleviate peak demand. The need for back-up, standby generators adds a cost layer to production, taking it further away from economic feasibility. The other major obstacle to wind generation is the storage problem. At present our ability to store electricity (in batteries) is rather inefficient so we cannot engineer a system that holds extra energy over time to balance things out. Energy not consumed during high capacity periods vanishes off the grid.

The potential up side of wind is too large to pass up, but the current strategy of local fossil fuel redundancy is grossly inefficient. Some proposed solutions seek to convert and store surplus wind energy in other forms. The U.S. Energy Department and Xcel have created a partnership to explore and attempt to make operational a system that uses surplus, off peak wind energy to split water for hydrogen.[120] The hydrogen would then be burned through a fuel cell to create electricity during peak hours (this process expends about half of the energy input). Another storage proposal envisions using surplus wind energy to pump air into enclosed spaces (for example underground caverns) so that the pressurized air could then be injected into natural gas generators which would otherwise use up their own energy to create pressurized air, cutting gas consumption by 40%.[121]

Both of wind's problems, variability and storage, point to the importance of an intelligent and universal grid system, a simpler and more efficient solution than these complex storage techniques. I am referring here to the distribution convergence and generation divergence mentioned at the top of this chapter. A large regional, even national, network of generation would allow every locality and every individual consumer to generate electricity according to their own comparative advantage. In places where wind is strong and siting conditions permit, only turbines need be installed. In places where solar radiation is strongest, only collectors are installed, and so on down the line for every one of the feasible and environmentally sound energy choices. The necessary redundancy is created by regional fluctuations in supply and demand (due to time zone, climate, and other differences) as well as by micro-generation (at the individual consumer level). When one part of the network is drawing larger loads than can be locally supplied, other parts of the network experiencing surpluses step in to fill the gap. The larger the network and the greater the number of generating options, the more consistent will be the energy supply. Storage is unnecessary since low output from one source is counterbalanced by unused energy from another. This grid system is more fully elaborated in a subsequent section. It is mentioned now only to highlight how problems of variability and storage (which arise in the context of many forms of energy creation) can be overcome by a systemic, comparative advantage approach which minimizes waste and capital expenditures.

As with each of the other energy modalities discussed here, wind energy technology is benefiting from research advances that are or will be soon making for even better rates of return. For instance, work being done with superconductors could lead to fantastically efficient generating motors.[122] Sound deafening technologies are removing one of the long held objections to turbine siting.[123] Geographic Information Systems (GIS) are illustrating ideal turbine placement for the reduction of bird flight collisions.[124] Advanced computer assisted design techniques, such as evolutionary computing, are perfecting and refining turbine design.

We may soon have radically different types of wind catchers such as vertical turbines that require less working area, making rooftop installation as common and easy as installing a solar panel, especially in urban settings where building heights replace the needs for towers.[125] Offshore wind farms are also an important application that could expand wind derived energy to even higher levels.

Solar

Potential Supply: 100% (of 2006 levels)126

Solar power is a tantalizing prospect. The energy is everywhere, free for the taking, and clean. The amount of sunlight reaching Earth's surface is 6,000 times the amount of energy used by all human beings worldwide.[127] The total amount of fossil fuel used by humans since the start of civilization is equivalent to less than 30 days of sunshine.[128] The problem is that we have not always been able to convert this energy effectively. The solar to electricity conversion rate for the best silicon solar panels stands at about 18–20% (the rest is lost as heat). Green plants use photosynthesis to convert about 25% of photosynthetically active solar radiation into chemical power.[129] In December 2006 the NREL announced that 40.7% solar to electricity efficiency has been achieved using concentrated solar panels (CSPs) made of multijunction, gallium arsenide cells.[130] Solar concentration is done using carefully placed mirrors or other reflective materials to focus the light. One form of CSP technology, also called thermal CSP, uses mirrors to focus the energy towards a gas enclosed tube and then uses the heated gas to create steam and then spin a turbine. A newer type of CSP trains light energy towards the solar cell region of the panel, producing an electron flow and electricity. Newer CSP panels, such as the ones announced by the NREL, revolutionize the solar cells as well, moving away from traditional single layer, silicon films: multijunction technology consists of a layering of the solar cell so that layers of different materials capture varying parts of the spectrum more effectively. More recent advances, including nanotube based cells, are refining this concept so that an even larger band of the spectrum triggers a photoelectric effect as the light passes through. Even the idea of solar panels has been shattered by the new polymer based inks that can be printed anywhere to create solar generation from any available surface. All the new technologies lessen the silicon content of the panels, thereby greatly reducing their cost (and also helping to prevent silicon shortages).

Solar energy has the potential to become the number one energy source for the entire world using existing technologies. A recent calculation showed that covering just .5% of the world's hottest deserts with CSPs could provide 100% of the world's electricity (and this was using the older thermal CSP technology).[131] This study also recommends that future transmission of renewable electricity be conducted along a high voltage direct current (HVDC) grid in order to minimize transmission efficiency losses over long distances (DC transmission loses about 3% per 1000 kilometers, AC transmission losses are higher; see grid discussion below).

If solar energy's potential is so vast, then why are we not charging full steam ahead with solar production? The main reasons up to now have been the large receiving surface area required and the variability of solar insolation. Much like the wind energy problem discussed above, a commitment to solar energy requires redundancy with fossil fuel backup generators (current CSP farms require about 27% fossil fuel generation at night).[132] As for the physical footprint of solar farms, newer technologies vastly reduce surface area requirements and the proposed use of HVDC transmission would allow for the placement of solar farms in unused desert areas (with minimal ecological impact). Until recently cost has also been a prohibitive factor since silicon based cells could not compete with traditional generation. Newer systems have drastically reduced the amount of silicon needed and also the manufacturing costs so that power derived from thermal CSP runs about $50 per barrel of oil equivalent—with a cost of $20 per barrel expected from mass production.[133] Finally, a new technique known as trigeneration goes over the top as far as energy efficiency. Sometimes called CHCP (Combined Heat Cooling and Power), this type of power plant combines a thermal CSP plant with the production of hot water and air cooling capabilities, reaching 90% or higher energy conversion efficiencies.[134] First the CSP is used to create steam to power turbines and make electricity, then, as the steam cools and becomes water, it can be diverted for use as hot water, or into an absorption cooler that creates cold air for air-conditioning and refrigeration. The potential uses for trigeneration are especially important for industrial plants whose remote location prevents a grid connection, for individual commercial buildings, and also for individual residential installations where a complete heating, cooling, and electric system could be run from locally installed CSPs. It should be noted that CHCP can drastically improve the efficiency of any form of thermal generation (which would include fossil fuels, nuclear fission and fusion, biomass, and hydrogen) and should be highly encouraged wherever feasible. Provided that a grid system is in place, allowing for efficient long distance transmission and the elimination of back up fossil fuel plants, then there is no place to go but up for solar energy (at least in places that enjoy a comparative advantage in solar radiation). Scaled down solar technology is also easy to use and maintain and has enormous potential as a micro-generation technology. Individual consumers can become their own trigeneration power plants, supplying their own needs and, during periods of surplus, selling their generation to others on the grid.

Geothermal

Potential Supply: 10% (of 2006 levels)135

Geothermal energy is a potentially important and untapped source of clean energy. Geothermal generation consists of bringing superheated water from deep inside the Earth up to the surface for use in thermal generation. Anyone who has seen a geyser has seen geothermal steam energy at work. At one time this resource was thought to be fairly limited geographically. Newer techniques, known collectively as Enhanced (or engineered) Geothermal Systems (EGS), allow for energy to be extracted from a much wider range of geological formations and steam sources, creating a much larger resource. The heat source for geothermal energy is the Earth's core, and, although a particular geothermal field cannot be said to be strictly speaking renewable, the global supply of EGS resource is thought to be sufficient to supply global needs for thousands of years. This resource is also available, in varying degrees of intensity, under landmasses throughout the globe.

According to a recent feasibility study, if fully exploited, U.S. geothermal resources could provide up to 100 GW of capacity by 2050.[136] This is approximately 10% of the electrical energy generated today in the U.S. and is not subject to fuel depletion and air pollution concerns. Furthermore, geothermal plants have very small physical footprints and can be sited almost anywhere. Geothermal is also scalable down to the individual building or residential user and as a source of thermal energy can be used for trigeneration. Finally, there are indications that CO_2 could be used as reservoir heat-transfer fluid in the geothermal extraction process, providing another useful form of CO_2 sequestration.[137]

The challenge for geothermal energy is the complexity of finding and gaining access to the resource. These tasks have been made easier by advances in drilling techniques (largely borrowed from oil and gas drilling) and greater geologic data. With an investment of about one billion dollars over the next 15 years, the target of 100 GW by 2050 is achievable according to a recent MIT study.[138] This is less than the cost of one new, clean coal power plant.

This study did not include the potential of ocean geothermal generation. Ocean geothermal generation, currently at the experimental stage, involves the use of temperature gradients in sea water to run turbines.[139]

Land based geothermal energy is essentially clean, although small amounts of non condensable gases (CO_2, H_2S, methane, hydrogen, sulfur dioxide and ammonia) can be released if certain techniques are used. A closed-loop binary system returns the source geofluid stream in its entirety to the Earth and no gases are released. Depending on the type of geological formations being mined for heat, there exists the possibility of a substantial water demand in geothermal production. Unless a process for using sequestered CO_2 as the transfer fluid is developed, the water requirements could be a limiting factor in some cases.[140]

Waste Biomass

Potential Supply: 8.6% (of 2005 levels)141

Biomass energy is everything from throwing another log on the fire, to making ethanol or heating oil from corn stalks, to making heating oil from sewage, to combusting food and agricultural wastes as fuel sources for thermoelectric generation. Biomass can consist of waste materials from industry, agriculture, forestry, and households or can be grown specifically to create energy (such as with corn, soybeans, seed oils, jatropha, and algal oils). There are two main end products from biomass processing: fuels and gases. Using biomass to create biofuels is discussed below in the transportation and heating oil section. Here we look solely at the use of biomass as a source of fuel for generating electricity from gas. All together, biomass supplies 47% of all renewable energy consumed in the U.S. (six times more than wind, solar, and geothermal combined).[142] The energy content of global biomass production is estimated to be around eight times the total annual consumption of energy from all sources. At present the world uses about 7% of its biomass production.[143]

Most people associate waste to energy biomass systems with the old incinerating technologies of the late 20th century. These dirty technologies were fraught with hazardous emissions such as dioxins and furans. The new processes for converting waste into energy use entirely different methods and offer a small but crucial avenue for energy production. Their advantage comes largely due to their complementary benefits in the area of waste disposal (discussed in Waste, below), but since they are also involved in energy creation they are included in this section.

How much energy are we talking? Projected data from one pilot facility using plasma arc technology (see below for details on this process) suggest that every ton of MSW produces approximately 1.4KWh net electricity, 330.69 lbs. of slag, and 11.023 lbs. of sulfur (both the slag and sulfur are commercially viable products).[144] Since the electricity is generated via a syngas turbine (see earlier discussion of syngas), there still needs to be a CO_2 capture mechanism. If multiplied across the U.S. 2005 MSW stream,[145] the approximately 245.7 million Tons of MSW could be producing 343.9 billion kWh of electricity, 40.61 million Tons of slag, 1.35 million Tons of sulfur. This amounts to 8.6% of the 2005 electricity generated in the U.S.[146] Since this is a net amount one needs to add to this the parasitic energy consumed by the process to arrive at an even higher total production. The amount of MSW entering the system would be reduced if recycling programs divert part of the waste stream.

From the perspective of cost, if a new waste biomass plant costs $250 million, and tipping fees for landfilling waste are $80/ton, then the plant breaks even in less than 4½ years.[147] At $50/ton then the time frame is less than seven years. These calculations do not include transportation cost savings, landfill emissions capture savings, the additional cost of CO_2 sequestration, or income from the sale of surplus syngas and/or electricity, sulfur, and slag. Clearly the economics of waste biomass are favorable. For urban centers with a large waste stream, high tipping fees, and high electricity costs, the potential benefits are redoubtable. In view of these advantages, it behooves us all to become more familiar with some of the terms and technologies connected with biomass generation:

Solid Recovered Fuel (SRF): SRF is derived from waste materials such as Municipal Solid Waste (MSW), agricultural wastes, and sewage waste byproducts. MSW can be subjected to a process called Mechanical Heat Treatment or autoclaving, whereby the inorganic portion is separated out before the organic portion is thermally reduced to SRF pellets. SRF can be used as a combustion fuel in place of coal in a coal fired generating plant. Some newer plants allow for the mixing of fuel types (co-firing), including SRF. In urban areas, SRF can be the largest available renewable energy resource due to the large and constant stream of wastes being produced. The same constraints on greenhouse gas emissions apply to SRF fired generation. A standardized world market for SRF could provide a strong incentive for developing nations to process, use, and sell their biomass instead of disposing of waste in less desirable manners.

Pyrolysis: This technique involves the thermal degradation of waste in the absence of air, producing char, oil, and syngas. Pyrolysis requires dry biomass waste and is therefore limited in scope. Recently, pyrolysis has been signaled as an effective means of carbon sequestration if the remaining char is used as a long term soil amendment. The so-called agrichar is able to boost plant yields and reduce fertilizer use so this method is not only a means of producing energy and reducing solid waste, but also of improving agricultural performance. Char used for personal use combustion, a practice common in many developing nations, would not count as carbon sequestration. One pyrolysis caveat: concerns about toxic dioxin and furan emissions persist with this technology and require a determinative, objective study.

Thermal Deploymerization (TPD): This process is a form of pyrolysis that does not require dry biomass fuels, thus saving considerable energy expense. It can also be termed hydrous pyrolysis. TPD plants that are designed to consume manure only are called Thermochemical Conversion (TCC) plants. Those that can consume manure and vegetable wastes are called Thermal Conversion Process (TCP) plants. In general, TPD involves the combustion of the fuel under pressure and in the presence of calcium hydroxite (a product formed from lime and water). The creation of calcium hydroxite is itself an energy intensive, water consuming, and CO_2 emitting process whose demands need to be included in the TPD energy and emissions balances. TPD takes the biomass and transforms it into a light crude oil which is in turn refined into any number of liquid fuels.

Plasma Arc Gasification (PAG): Waste materials can also be turned into syngas (and electricity) using a technique called plasma arc gasification (PAG), a type of thermal gasification. Gasification in general involves the combustion of waste, but this time in the presence of air and usually at a higher temperature. PAG systems are very high heat treatments that turn their waste fuel into syngas and slag (an inert, vitreous material that can be used in construction). The plasma arc process literally rips apart everything in its path into basic elemental gases. Although the process is energy parasitic, a small positive net production is achieved from the derived syngas. An 85 tons per day test facility is scheduled for completion in May 2007 in Ottawa, Canada[148] and the first such system in the U.S. is scheduled for 2009 in Florida.[149] These projects should be watched closely.

What is nice about PAG is that it can indiscriminately handle any type of waste, wet or dry, hazardous or not, except nuclear. It can process biomass waste and inorganic materials, including metals, plastics, electronics, chemicals, and glass. It can be used not only to process current waste, but also to retro-process landfill material, thereby returning these areas to their natural state. PAG is the currently used technology to dispose of medical wastes and hazardous waste materials from Superfund sites. Another cost cutting option is to tie in the PAG plant with an existing coal or oil based plant. The treatment of gases is the same in all three plants and the gas treatment part of the process constitutes about half of the PAG plant construction costs.[150]

The exploitation of biomass represents one of the most important avenues of renewable energy since it is a resource continuously produced by human activity and would otherwise contribute to a growing and serious waste management problem. As SRF, biomass is not clean (although it is cleaner than fossil fuels) and needs to be regulated. As a fuel for pyrolysis or gasification, biomass burns more cleanly (each particular technique produces a mix of different byproducts).

Biomass to electricity is unlikely to assume the overall importance of solar energy in the global mix, but it is an important and irreplaceable niche source for the waste reduction reasons noted above.

Biogas

Potential Supply: Unknown

Biogas is a methane rich gas created from the decomposition of organic materials. It can occur naturally in the form of swamp gas and marsh gas and is also produced by landfills. From the perspective of the future environmental economy, biogas is produced from sewage decomposition in an anaerobic reactor. Biogas can be cleaned of impurities to form Renewable Natural Gas (RNG) which can be compressed to form Compressed Natural Gas (CNG). In these two forms, biogas is completely compatible with all natural gas pipeplines, appliances, and engines.[151] Biogas production is an important byproduct of sewage treatment in places where sewage sludge is converted into fertilizer (discussed in Waste, below) and is an important niche product in the field of waste processing.

ENERGY CONVERSION: TRANSPORTATION AND HOME HEATING

	Mass Density (MJ/kg)	Volume Density (MJ/L)
Compressed Gaseous Hydrogen (700 bar)[153]	120	9
Compressed Natural Gas (200 bar)[154]	53.6	10
Methane Gas[155]	50	21
Polyethylene Plastic[156]	46.3	42.6
Gasoline[157]	44	31
Residential Heating Oil[158]	44	34
Biodiesel[159]	42.2	30.53
Butanol[160]	37.5	29.91
Ethanol[161]	37	21
Anthracite Coal[162]	31	69.06
Compressed Syngas (200 bar)[163]	<26	Not Available
Methanol[164]	20.16	15.91
Cow Dung[165]	15.5	Not Available
Lithium Ion Battery[166]	.792	Not Available
Lead Acid Battery[167]	.079	Not Available

Table 4 : Common Energy Densities *Data Source: Endnotes: 152, 153, 154, 155, 156, 157, 158, 159, 160, 161, 162, 163, 164, 165, 166, 167 (larger version of this table available here: http://image.xyvy.info/Table4.jpg)*

As currently structured, transportation and home heating (using heating oil or steam) are separate components of the energy system, unconnected to the electrical grid. My view of an ideal energy economy is one where all work is done by electricity supplied by the grid or by micro-generation (*i.e.*, distributed energy). In such a world the need for liquid fuels in transportation and home heating would be reduced nearly to zero. In the meantime though we must envisage a world in transition where liquid fuels will continue to have a role to play.

Liquid fuels are portable forms of energy storage that allow us to individualize storage and consumption. Apart from the gases, they happen to be the most efficient forms of storage at present (see Table 4). This quality is measured by the energy density or amount of energy stored in a given space per unit of mass or volume. The gases pose the problem of their low volume densities, meaning that a large volume of the gas needs to be collected to achieve the higher mass densities. What the numbers on Table 4 are saying is that, by weight, biodiesel holds an energy store comparable to gasoline and home heating oil and a larger one than coal, butanol, ethanol, and methanol. These number also show that battery energy densities are far from those achieved by other forms of storage, suggesting that liquid fuels will continue to dominate the transportation and home heating sectors.

These numbers also reveal that biodiesel and butanol hold the greatest promise as far as the big four bio-fuels (biodiesel, butanol, ethanol, methanol) go. Being non-water soluble fuels, biodiesel and butanol hold an advantage over ethanol and methanol in that existing pipelines and trucks can be used for its transport. Biodiesel can also be used as a substitute for heating oil. Especially for this last reason, biodiesel would seem to me to be the best choice for the role of primary liquid fuel until we are weaned entirely from the liquid fuel economy. From the point of view of greenhouse emissions, this view is substantiated by the EPA's fuel comparison (Table 5) which shows that except for the possibility of cellulosic ethanol (and it is not clear if delivery infrastructure costs are included here), biodiesel provides the best net emissions benefits.

Replacement Fuel	Change in GHG Emissions	Replacement Fuel	Change in GHG Emissions
Cellulosic Ethanol	-91%	Corn Ethanol	-22%
Biodiesel	-68%	Liquified Petroleum Gas	-20%
Sugar Ethanol	-56%	Methanol	-9%
Electricity	-47%	Coal to Liquids (/w Carbon Capture and Storage)	+4%
Gaseous Hydrogen	-41%	Liquid Hydrogen	+7%
Compressed Natural Gas	-29%	Gas to Liquid Diesel	+9%
Liquified Natural Gas	-23%	Coal to Liquids (/w out Carbon Capture and Storage)	+119%

Table 5 : Estimated Change in Green House Gas Emissions if Petroleum Replaced. **Note:** Includes emissions from fossil extraction, feedstock growth and distribution. Averaged for the different methods of producing the fuels. *Data Source: Environmental Protection Agency.* (larger version of this table available here: http://image.xyvy.info/Table5.jpg)

I am not sure which of the biodiesel feedstocks was considered here (most likely soybean oil). If one were to apply one of the higher oil yield feedstocks such as algae oil, then biodiesel probably overtakes cellulosic ethanol for the top spot. Finally, the finding of a negative 47% change in GHG by switching to electricity is most probably based on electricity production without carbon capture and sequestration (CCS). Assuming CCS, the use of electricity as a vehicular fuel source would likely shift that result into a position ahead of both cellulosic ethanol and biodiesel for the top position. Unfortunately cellulosic butanol is not included in this chart, but one can presume its effects would be comparable to cellulosic ethanol.

Biofuel Biomass

Biofuels are biomass converted into liquid energy. Although there are experts who advocate for butanol, biodiesel and ethanol have assumed the leadership in this category.

Ethanol

Ethanol has gained prominence due to its promotion of several agricultural feedstocks, mainly corn, sugar cane, and soybeans. In fact ethanol can be produced from any biomass containing sugar using a fermentation process similar to that of creating distilled beverage spirits. A major question with the ethanol economy is whether it benefits energy and environmental needs, or just the profit bottom line of agribusinesses. Due to varying efficiencies, the choice of feedstock makes a huge difference as to the net energy balance (whether one winds up with more energy than it takes to make) and the overall net environmental gains (reductions of overall pollutants minus increases in fertilizer, pesticide, and water use) in converting to ethanol. When one takes into account the energy, emissions, and water costs of feedstock production, there is still some controversy whether corn barely breaks even or actually require more energy to produce than is gained.[167] Sugar cane does better, but only in places such as Brazil and Colombia, where the Sun shines long and hard throughout the year.

Much current research is being conducted on the possibilities of deriving ethanol from cellulose as opposed to the plant starch. This would allow a large amount of waste material such as corn stalks, bagasse, grasses, and even wood to be converted into fuel. Some of the techniques being tested involve bioengineering a variety of microbes into fuel making machines. A breakthrough in the creation of cellulosic ethanol could change the efficiencies and economic balance in favor of greater ethanol production. In the meantime, the huge infrastructure requirements (completely separate pipeline and distribution network) and opportunity costs for food agriculture seem to weigh against this option. Furthermore, and this is a problem with all agriculturally based energy, there exists the danger of deforestation and other types of environmental degradation as a side effect of the rush to produce more plant material.

As a final note, the production process of biodiesel from vegetable oils (see below) requires an alcohol such as ethanol or methanol. These alcohol fuels have other industrial and agricultural uses as well, so that even if the policy decision is made to move towards a biodiesel economy there will still continue to exist a growing demand for ethanol and methanol. For this reason, I would encourage the continued, if not moderated, expansion of the bioethanol industry, keeping in mind a more moderate long term demand for the product.

Butanol

Butanol is very similar to ethanol in that both are alcohols made by fermenting biomass. There are some significant differences though that lend credence to the assertion that butanol is a better choice than ethanol as a liquid fuel. First there is the fact that the microörganisms that convert biomass to butanol are capable of processing cellulose.[168] Since cellulosic ethanol is often touted as the holy grail of liquid fuels, it seems strange that butanol is so overlooked in research and policy forecasting. Secondly, butanol does not pose the same water contamination problems as ethanol which means that existing pipeline infrastructure could be used and fewer fuel blending problems are likely to arise. Third, butanol can be mixed at a higher ratio than ethanol with gasoline for existing cars. This has been reported as up to 85% without engine modification.[169] Fourth, existing ethanol plants can be retrofitted feasibly for butanol production. The one disadvantage is butanol's lower octane ratings. A higher octane means that an engine can run at a higher compression and therefore more efficiently. This is compensated somewhat by butanol's slightly higher energy density (see Table 4). That butanol is a legitimate option is attested to by the current joint venture between Dupont and BP to manufacture biobutanol in the United Kingdom.[170] We can expect biobutanol to be commercially available starting in around 2010.

Biodiesel

To the extent that we must continue to abide by a liquid fuel based transportation sector, the preferred choice is biodiesel. Not only because of its higher energy density and ease of infrastructure transition, but also due to its fungibility with home heating oil. As with ethanol, a wide discrepancy exists between crop feedstocks for biodiesel. On a pure energy density basis, drawing from the data in Tables 4 and 6 and the fact that ethanol from corn is produced at an average rate of 372.6 gallons per acre,[171] any crop that produces at least 257 gallons per acre of biodiesel would be yielding the approximately the same volume efficiency as ethanol from corn. The productivity and chemical properties of feedstocks are also subject to advances in genetic engineering that could perfect these crops dramatically.[172]

Problems often raised with biodiesel include its cold weather performance and its proclivity to oxidize and polymerize (harden). These tendencies vary according to the type of feedstock used to create the oil.[173] While posing challenges, the negative properties of pure biodiesel can be overcome by blending, additives, or engine modifications.[174] The history of fossil fuels is replete with engineered blending; the biodiesel industry will experience the same improvements once it acquires market momentum. For instance, a new technology called Centia has been recently introduced that produces a biodiesel with petrodiesel properties.[175] Biodiesel-Butanol blends could also give better cold weather performance. Last but far from least, a new 'dual fuel' system created by SAE Energy is radically boosting the overall performance qualities of biodiesel (possibly including cold weather performance) by injecting either natural gas or hydrogen into the air intake of the diesel engine (see Syngas, Dual Fuel, and H2CAR below).

Crop	Oil Production (gal/acre)
Corn	18
Cotton	35
Soybean	48
Pumpkin Seed	57
Safflower Seed	83
Sunflower Seed	102
Peanuts	113
Jatropha	202
Avocado	282
Coconut Oil	287
Oil Palm	635
Algae[180]	5,000

Table 6 : Selected Biodiesel Feedstocks Data Source: see endnotes: 178, 179
(larger version of this table available here: http://image.xyvy.info/Table6.jpg)

A renewed interest in algal oils is becoming evident.[176] The U.S. Department of Energy ran a research project on the use of algae oil for biodiesel in the 1980s and 90s, but further work was abandoned due to a drop in fossil fuels prices.[177] The DOE study determined that 28,000 km² or 0.3% of the land area of the U.S. could be utilized to produce enough biodiesel from algae oil to replace all transportation fuel needs for the entire country as of that time. Algal oils possess favorable cold weather properties and less favorable polymerization properties.[178] One of the more interesting integrated concepts involves the use of algal reactors as carbon sequestration chambers for the production of biodiesel.[179] To the extent that this CO_2 is coming from non-renewable sources, it continues to be a non-renewable when combusted as biodiesel, but it would certainly stretch the energy to emissions ratio from the same original fossil source. Biodiesel from agricultural crop sources is a renewable resource since no new atmospheric carbon is released in the process.

As interesting as biodiesel, butanol, and possibly a cellulosic ethanol appear to be, it cannot be forgotten that to the extent they are renewable and do not add atmospheric carbon, neither do they reduce carbon levels. Since we may well face the need to not only stabilize, but also to reduce GHG levels. We should be exploring ways of capturing emissions from all sources, including at the individual tailpipe and boiler levels. From time to time there have appeared glimpses of this idea[180] which should be a major focus of research until such time as atmospheric levels are within historically acceptable ranges and a true zero emissions economy has been achieved. Some of the newer materials for smokestack CO_2 sequestration could be scaled down for single engine emissions and the captured CO_2 used as a valuable commodity as discussed in the climate section above.

Syngas, Dual Fuel, and H2CAR

Syngas is an important precursor to alternative liquid fuels due to its role in the Fischer-Tropsch process, the product of which can be refined into any of the liquid fuels, or synbiofuels. It will be recalled from earlier sections that syngas is produced in clean coal IGCC plants as well as in plasma arc gasifiers. Syngas can also be produced from methane, whose sources include landfills, anaerobic sewage digestion, and methyl hydrate fields. Syngas may also be converted into Synthetic Natural Gas which can be used in place of, or in addition to, natural gas with no modification of infrastructure or appliances (although its energy density is of a slightly lower level). Syngas products coming from coal gasification are not renewable since their carbon source is the original coal material. Syngas coming from waste is partially renewable (food, timber, and agricultural wastes) and partially not (plastics). Syngas from methane is not renewable. As an intermediary compound derived from a number of materials, syngas could play an important role in a growing synbiofuel industry.

One of the more promising prospects for the transportation sector, the dual fuel engine, is being currently implemented by SAE Energy159.1 in the U.S. By drawing natural gas, synthetic natural gas, or hydrogen into the biofuel line, thereby creating a mixed fuel, the engine's biofuel consumption is reduced by 50%, its GHG emissions are reduced by 50%, its fuel efficiency improves by 50%, and horsepower jumps 200% or more. The limitations of producing hydrogen, discussed below, still apply to this system, but the anticipated availability of synthetic natural gas and methane (especially from ocean methyl hydrates) makes this an interesting transition phase fuel mix.

Another variation on this theme comes from a recent National Academy of Sciences paper that proposes a biomass to liquids method for producing enough liquid fuel to supply the entire transportation sector in the U.S. while using 40% less biomass than the other biofuels discussed above. In a process similar to Fischer-Tropsch, carbon derived from biomass plus hydrogen derived using renewable energy are fed into a gasifier to produce any type of liquid hydrocarbon desired (different catalysts produce different fuels). Cars using this fuel will still emit CO_2, but since the source of the carbon is biomass, it would be considered a carbon neutral emission. This process is essentially a way of suppressing or sequestering the CO_2 normally formed during the gasification of carbon containing materials and then using the carbon as a storage hold for hydrogen. Thus is overcome the fuel cell battery and hydrogen transport problems. The authors of this paper have named the process H2CAR and it could be a very important contribution to the future of liquid fuels.[181] They argue that "it is a better utilization of land to generate electricity or hydrogen from solar cells or an alternative carbon-free energy source and use biomass as a carbon source to store this energy as synthetic fuels" than to simply generate electricity or produce hydrogen from biomass.[182] They conclude that the process presents an intriguing possibility of the United States becoming a net exporter of oil.

Hydrogen

As the most abundant element in the universe (and on Earth), hydrogen would seem to be a logical choice for energy storage. While the technologies currently exist to power vehicles using hydrogen fuel cells there are several large obstacles to surmount: 1) The cost of producing fuel cells (needed to replace the internal combustion engine in vehicles; 2) the energy costs of producing hydrogen; 3) the need for and cost of pressurizing hydrogen (due to the low volumetric energy density, a large volume is required); and 4) the need for an entirely new storage and transportation infrastructure. For these reasons, hydrogen is viewed as a worthwhile fuel choice for long term development but not for immediate use. Once we are able to resolve the challenges of fossil fuel and renewable energies than the energy cost issues raised by the hydrogen economy are overcome. If we are able to resolve these other challenges, however, then the need for a transition to hydrogen are also diluted unless the battery storage problem remains refractory and the electric car remains unworkable. In the latter case then the H2CAR method of hydrogen storage appears closer at hand than compressed hydrogen storage in a dual fuel or pure fuel cell system.

ENERGY CONVERSION: DISTRIBUTION OF ELECTRICITY

As I have been elaborating all along, the only way to move into the renewable economy, and the redundancy required by intermittent energy sources, is to convert gradually into a distribution system that allows geographic and temporal equalization across the system.[183] I have described this as distribution convergence and production divergence. The system becomes in essence an electrical internet where any consumer can buy power from any producer and individuals can produce and distribute their own electricity via net metering. This system allows alternative renewable plants to be sited where they are most productive and to then supply consumers anywhere in the country. Electricity becomes the universal form of energy, allowing for convergence of industrial, residential, climate control, and transportation uses.[184] The price for the electricity is the average of all input costs plus a preset profit lodestar that rewards lower cost production, and every consumer pays the same price. Each producer receives its costs plus a profit pegged to cost efficiency (*i.e.*, the lower the cost of the energy, the greater the profit margin) while each consumer benefits from a cost average. For long distance runs, high voltage direct current (HVDC) minimizes efficiency losses while newer wiring technologies involving a central cooling superconductor would allow the same wire diameter to carry much larger loads.[185] However, distribution losses will seem far less important when the source of the energy is free. Finally, to avoid service interruptions, distribution wiring is conducted by underground conduits in places where weather and other mechanically based transmission failures are a risk. The rising output from co-generation on the local, micro-regional, and individual levels will not only maximize redundancy and support local economies, but will also reduce the risk of wire or connection based interruptions.

FREQUENTLY ASKED QUESTIONS

What should be our priorities for the new energy economy?

Having zipped through the energy landscape in this fashion now allows us to make a priority chart for future action on energy. To make this clearer, the above information can be formed into a flow chart of preferred options (all percentages are based on 2005 consumption levels): 1) maximize use of solar, wind, geothermal, and natural hydro (tidal, current, and wave) until we achieve maximization: wind-20%, geothermal-10%, natural hydro-10%, waste biomass-8% and solar (both concentrated and multijunction)-52%; require distribution convergence, production divergence, and distribution efficiency, 2) encourage local and individual micro-generation and implement net metering everywhere, 3) maximize efficiency of power generation by opting for trigeneration (CHCP) or cogeneration (CHP) at macro and micro levels whenever feasible, 4) maximize production of biodiesel from biomass using syngas reformation, 5) make new vehicles and public carriers as biodiesel hybrids and then dual fuel biodiesel hybrids using natural gas, 6) continue a vigorous R & D program for Carbon Capture and Sequestration (CCS) applications whether from renewable sources or not, including sequestration from individual tail pipes and boilers, opting for productive uses of CO_2 over simple burial; apply CSS as soon as possible to all existing sources, including vehicle emissions, 7) continue a vigorous R & D program for the development of the H2CAR and natural gas from methyl hydrates processes, 8) ramp up coal and gas to biodiesel or H2CAR biomass to biodiesel production when either CSS solutions or H2CAR technologies are operational, 9) continue a vigorous R & D program for biodiesel production from algae oil, 10) continue a vigorous R & D program for improving the energy density of electric car batteries, 11) continue a vigorous R & D program to develop Hydrogen production using renewable energies, 12) continue a vigorous R & D program for Thorium based nuclear fission, and 13) continue a vigorous R & D program for strategies of atmospheric carbon capture.

How are we as a society going to move towards the new energy economy?

By establishing a public policy that: 1) sets forth a National Energy Policy that establishes priorities and allows decision making at all levels to contribute to the national priorities described in the above FAQ, 2) sets the economic conditions necessary for the energy transition. The crucial first steps towards the new energy economy involve sending the appropriate signals to energy markets—placing caps on greenhouse gas emissions or placing a price on CO_2

emissions as well as the elimination of subsidies to technologies and fuels that run contrary to the National Energy Policy. Placing caps (and allowing companies to trade emissions credits) is generally recognized as the preferred strategy by environmental economists, but is much more difficult to design and implement than a straight tax. CO_2 emission pricing is easiest to achieve by means of a carbon tax, an across the board tax on every type of activity that influences the atmospheric carbon balance, including electrical generation, deforestation, car emissions, agricultural and industrial production. In addition to boosting the economic viability of clean and renewable technologies, a carbon tax also helps to fund the research and development necessary to make a full energy transition. Carbon taxation should be used as an immediate, short term measure to be supplanted by a cap and trade system as soon as possible. The goal of this policy and research is to reach a point where we are able to provide unlimited renewable and clean energy for ourselves and to provide energy leadership and coöperation to the rest of the world.

FOREST LOSS AND AGRICULTURE

The planet is losing forests at a frightening rate.[186] Forests, and especially tropical forests, hold a large proportion of the biodiversity on the planet, and are also the main source of carbon capture. Unfortunately, a large part of the most important tropical forests lie in lesser developed nations where plain vanilla carpist[187] thinking often reigns supreme. These are the forests that contain the largest percentage of biodiversity and do the lion's share of carbon dioxide capture. What this means is that the developed countries need to view these forests as global resources and act accordingly. To put it more bluntly, to the extent that the people in these tropical forest countries do not receive a livable share of the world's income then the precious forest resources under their control will remain imperiled. Some economists have suggested that the best way to protect natural resources such as forests is to liberalize the industry, or industries, that depend on their management and preservation. In order to save the Amazon or Congo forests, one would want there to be a healthy timber industry for the local people to protect. This argument is based on the idea that when things are valueless then they are more likely to be disregarded and destroyed and is also at the base of the biodiversity convention discussed earlier.

The problem with this idea in practice has been that too often liberalization is accompanied by increased distributional inequities. Whether tilted towards large local or multinational owners, the result of the inequities is a market failure that defeats the goals of the strategy. Faced with such an injustice, growing numbers of small scale local people engage in illegal exploitation of the resource or sell out their interests to bigger players.[188] In both cases what often follows is migration to the cities or to more developed nations.[189] When one sees that major tropical forest nations such as Brazil, Colombia, Central African Republic, Guatemala and Honduras have Gini Indices[190] (a measure of distributional equity) of 58, 58.6, 61.3, 55.1, and 53.8 and that others such as the Congos, Gabon, Equatorial Guinea, Suriname, or French Guyana are not even covered by UN statistics, there is cause for grave concern.[191] Unless there is a government or traditional culture in place that is able to enforce a functioning form of distribution, the result will be mismanagement of the resource.[192] The second part of this problem is that many in the developed world have tended to view governmentally enforced distributional equity as an anti-free market practice, as tyranny, communism, and so on. For this reason, over the past century, it has been the policy of many developed nations to prop up and support regimes in these places that make minimal distributional demands on the profits from a given resource. The combined result of these conditions is global net forest loss, urbanization, and emigration.

Much forest loss is caused by clear-cutting for agricultural purposes. Given the pressure to produce economically it is understandable that many nations, especially impoverished ones, view this as a way out of under-development. From the environmentalist's perspective, the goal is to maximize the efficiency and minimize the impact of agricultural practices so that the rate of deforestation and its consequences be kept low. The single most important technological field of progress in this area is the creation of genetically modified (GMO) seeds and livestock. GMO seeds are engineered to be disease resistant cultivars of important economic crops that require less pesticides, less fertilizer, less irrigation, and are more productive. Similar advances are being made in animal livestock and aquaculture species. The engineering consists of splicing extraneous genes, either synthesized or obtained from another organism, into the target species genes. Genetic modification is not limited to food production; crops, animals, and bacteria are being modified to produce pharmaceuticals, chemicals, remediate toxic waste, and even biofuels. A related yet altogether different form of genetic intervention is known as radiation breeding where genetic material is shuffled randomly using radiation but no foreign genes are introduced.[193] As with anything new and scientific, GMO production has become hugely controversial around the world. Some lesser developed nations have embraced the technology wholeheartedly while others are resistant.[194]

One oft heard objection to transgenic products is that they are not safe to eat. This has never been shown to be true.[195] Food safety opponents rest their case largely on the lack of long term studies rather than evidence of actual harm.[196] Having determined that the known benefits outweigh the unknown risks, numerous countries have approved GMO crops for food and feedstocks.[197] Another problem raised is that these new frankenspecies will interbreed with their wild cousins and create new hybrids that are not able to survive in the wild.[198] This concern is supported by empirical evidence such as genetic studies of hybridization between cultured and wild salmon.[199] The precautionary principle suggests that approval of transgenic products be made contingent on the infertility of these organisms, thus rendering them unable to mix into the wild gene pool. A third concern arises from the dependency on biotech companies that these technologies could create on the part of developing nations and their farmers.[200] Terminator seeds that will not germinate unless a particular chemical is applied, or plants engineered to resist only pesticides manufactured by the biotech company, do create the danger of perpetuating a state of dependency on the part of developing nations. This brings the discussion once again to the question of technology transfer discussed previously in the context of biodiversity.

Technology transfer has always been a sticking point in global environmental policy. Technology owners believe they are entitled to a larger slice of the profit pie while those in control of the natural resource feel otherwise. Negotiations are slowly underway on the Agreement on Trade Related Aspects of Intellectual Property Rights (TRIPS) that could pave the way for greater application of environmentally sustainable technologies in developing countries.[201] The technologists need to bear in mind the consequences of an impasse, such as a more rapid degradation of common resources on which they too depend, a greater frequency of intellectual property theft, and weaker sales. Developed nations must accept, as a fact of life, that natural resource countries have a bargaining position that cannot be ignored or neglected. The owners of natural resources should recognize that technology is a factor of production like any other and must be assigned a profit share, but that technology, like all forms of intellectual property, is protected for a limited time. Fears of an endless dependency should be moderated in these countries by an understanding of and respect for international intellectual property law.

Apart from genetic engineering, one of the most interesting cutting edge areas of agricultural production is hydroponics. Hydroponics is agriculture without soil. Research is underway that could someday allow for subterranean or desert agriculture,[202] or high-rise building based agriculture in urban settings. The concept of converting otherwise infertile or unplantable areas of the planet to crop production could be the concept that ultimately saves our forests from an ever growing demand for surface area. One of the leading edge researchers in this field has proposed the construction of farm skyscrapers each of which could feed and hydrate 50,000 people per year.[203] Sewage treatment effluents and solid waste residues could serve important hydroponic functions as fertilizers. Enclosed agriculture also presents a potential means of carbon sequestration if CO_2 captured from fossil fuel combustion and other activities were to be circulated into these greenhouses, stimulating photosynthesis.

Agricultural production and carbon sequestration merge paths as well in an ancient agricultural technology due for a revival. Anthropologists have long been aware of the use of dark earth (i.e., *terra preta*) by indigenous Amazon peoples as away of improving soil quality in the jungle. Now soil scientists are discovering that this technique, generally known as agrichar, is not only an effective method of improving yields but is also an effective means of sequestering carbon and reducing fertilizer application.[204] Agrichar is a byproduct of biomass pyrolysis, a process with energy generation and waste management benefits (see Energy and Waste sections).

This glimpse into deforestation and its possible antidotes reveals a side of the environmental enigma that is often ignored, and a side of the new environmental economy, agritech, that is brimming with possibilities. This sector, including GMO development, hydroponics, and waste-to-nutrients research, is an essential component in the fight against biodiversity loss and climate change, and deserves the same budgetary and policy attention as alternative energy. The loss of forests poses a triple threat to the world's environment as a significant cause of global warming, biodiversity loss, and as a factor in the economic dislocation of large population masses. The rise of economic migration and urbanization in turn give impetus to the nasty demon of waste generation and disposal.

FREQUENTLY ASKED QUESTIONS

Should I use GMO foods?

The answer is a guarded yes. GMO foods hold much promise for lowering humanity's ecological footprint and should be encouraged by the consumer. The FDA has approved these foods for human consumption.[205] National agencies in other countries have reached similar conclusions. The main opposition to transgenic organisms is based on other concerns, not that they are harmful if eaten. These are the concerns that require scrutiny. The dangers of interference with wild stocks as well as of the perpetuation of trade imbalances based on technological dependence requires that this industry be regulated by global food and trade agencies. Political representatives should be encouraged to make GMO regulation part of their legislative agenda. The Union of Concerned Scientists offers a public forum for GMO policy information.[206]

Is there a way of evaluating forest products for their environmental impact?

The Forest Stewardship Council,[207] the Sustainable Forestry Initiative,[208] and the Programme for the Endorsement of Forest Certification[209] schemes are two of the most respected organizations certifying forestry operations. These organizations administer and supervise certification and labeling programs that allow consumers to verify whether forestry products are the result of the best environmental practices.

WASTE GENERATION

I prefer to think of waste as things we have not found a way to use yet. This may seem like a quixotic notion and I hope to dissuade you of this perception. Most waste experts say the best way to reduce waste is simply not to make any more of it. While the logic here is irrefutable, I find this strategy unreasonable and contrary to the needs of economic vitality. A stagnant economy can be just as urgent a threat to a healthy environment as a wasteful one. I do not foresee an abandonment of the economic ideals of growth, consumption, and technological improvement occurring anytime soon. To the contrary, the global economy seems to be moving in the opposite direction. I would therefore re-state the conventional waste policy addage 'reduce, re-use, recycle,' as 're-use, recycle,' since a world in which we sit around expending as little energy and utilizing as few new products as possible, just does not seem enticing or economically viable. Conventional notions of re-use and recycling won't do either, since as currently practiced they result in no more than a slowing down of the inevitable dumping. Due to degradation and error, the vast majority of recyclable materials end up as waste anyway. I vastly prefer the idea that we can continue to live life to the hilt as long as we think in new ways about how we fuel our activities, what materials we use, and then of how we re-use, recycle, or convert the byproducts of our activities. This approach has been called cradle-to-cradle thinking.[210] Converting cradle-to-cradle thinking into action requires us: a) to create a system of economic signals that send a clear message to businesses and consumers of the new and permanent policy direction, and b) to seek engineered solutions that cycle, integrate, and reuse services, processes and functions in a systemic way.

In the context of waste generation, the economic signaling that I am referring to boils down to the concept of pay-to-throw-away. Heretofore we have become accustomed to a system that allows us to dispose of as much as we want of any kind of waste for essentially the same price. To the average consumer of solid waste services, for example, no matter how much trash he or she places on the sidewalk, the price is the same. The same does not hold true for the municipality that pays for carting, landfilling, or other disposal by weight. The signal that more trash really does cost more is not getting through to the consumer. Sometimes the cost signal will be further vitiated by the availability of inexpensive, foreign sources of landfilling. A large amount of electronic waste for instance winds up being shipped by barge to Western Africa and India only to be stuffed into their distant landfills. Low cost disposal options encourage consumers to discard freely without a second thought to minimization, reuse, or recycling.

The effect is just like sweeping the dirt under the carpet. Sooner or later something will have to be done by the sweeper (or his successors) no matter how far away the waste is flung. Toxic chemicals that leach out from our distantly landfilled trash into distant waterways may wind up in our foods, in our waters, in our soils one day. We cannot continue to view distance as a barrier to pollution from waste since ultimately we all depend on the services provided by global commons such as air, water, and soil. Furthermore, over the long term, landfill space will become scarcer and more expensive. Other uses such as agriculture, habitation, wilderness preservation, recreation, and resource extraction will take priority. This is all part and parcel of the signaling failure. We simply do not pay the true costs of solid waste disposal, and even less so when the waste is disposed far away.

I recently reviewed the U.S. Department of Energy's estimation of renewable energy resources around the U.S. and was intrigued to discover that one of the best renewable resources available to New York City is bio-mass.[211] Waste biomass is anything organic that we throw away and includes most kitchen wastes, paper, plant matter, and sewage waste. This brought to light the essential fact about waste, that we need to start looking at these materials as if they were a valuable commodity, which they are. These materials, in addition to several forms of manmade waste that are not biomass, such as plastics, should be seen as a fuel for energy purposes. The amount of biomass disposal in large urban areas cannot support 100 percent of the energy needs in these places, but can become an important part of the mix, especially when one considers the avoidance of disposal needs.

Waste to Energy is not a new idea, but it is one place where technological progress can and will come to the rescue. Most people associate Waste To Energy (WTE) with the dioxin and furan-forming experience of incinerators from the 1990s.[212] The next wave of WTE is a completely different technology. The basic process is ultra high temperature gasification, the same technology used today to dispose of hazardous wastes at Superfund sites. The process burns the waste fuel at temperatures hotter than the Sun, splitting the molecules apart into energy rich gases that can be used to generate electricity. The only remaining solid is an inert glass like substance that can be formed into building and road materials. The new breed of WTE plants begin with a load of undifferentiated solid waste (including sewage sludge), then separate and divert the recylables, grind what remains, and then gasify the waste, producing electricity in the process. The plant can be located anywhere since no emissions or run off is produced. The process can handle every type of waste except nuclear. Plasma arc gasification, as this process is called, should be viewed primarily as a form of waste disposal that has as an added benefit a net energy surplus.

Opponents of WTE often point to the fact that recycling is more energy and waste efficient than gasification. I could not agree more. I still adhere to re-use and recycling as being higher and better uses than conversion to energy. That is why I mentioned that these plants will include a pre-treatment option. A process known as Mechanical Biological Treatment (MBT) eliminates the need for pre-sorting.[213] All household, commercial, unusable sewage sludge, and agricultural waste goes in to MBT. The inorganic fraction (metals, glass, plastic or just metals and glass) is mechanically separated for recycling using conveyors, industrial magnets, eddy current separators, trommels, shredders and other tailor made systems.[214] The remaining organic waste is subjected to partial anaerobic digestion to produce sewage plant power and ethanol (for biodiesel production) and also to secondary aerobic composting for fertilizer production. Methane released during the waste processing and disposal is captured and burned for internal power needs. What remains is then subjected to plasma arc gasification. The process is streamlined and integrated under one roof. The time consuming, and often error ridden, task of manual separation of recyclables will no longer be necessary. Sewage waste byproducts that can be used as fertilizers or mulch should also continue to be put to those higher uses rather than dumped into MBT. In the alternative, the entire solid waste stream can be processed via plasma arc gasification.

Now that we have seen how solid wastes may be managed, I turn to sewage waste. One of the most shameful conditions of life in the earliest 21st century is the fact that an enormous number of the world's inhabitants continue to dump raw sewage directly into natural waterways.[215] Longstanding traditions indicate that, in the past, the waterways have been able to process human waste adequately. Things are different now. Not only the quantity has changed, but also the nature of the waste. Increasingly, our waste consists of synthetic chemicals, pharmaceuticals, fertilizers, pesticides, and cosmetics, many of these designed to resist biodegradation or to interact with and alter animal tissues. Human debris is everywhere in the waterways, turning them into inhospitable chemical cocktails. The contamination not only threatens wildlife in these waters, but poses an even more direct threat to humans by depriving more and more people of safe drinking water. More than a billion people worldwide lack access to safe drinking water and 40 percent lack basic water sanitation.[216] It is imperative that we devise effective and cost efficient ways of dealing with our sewage treatment and that these methods be adopted around the world. Even treated sewage poses threats stemming from the concentration of nutrients, such as nitrogen, in the treated effluent and the inability of many systems to remove inorganic chemicals from the stream.

The two main priorities for sewage treatment are the prevention of toxics and nutrients from reaching the environment and the recovery of nutrients as fertilizers for agricultural or aquacultural purposes. After these two priorities have been addressed then energy uses of the waste stream should be considered. There are several research findings in the recent literature that point towards the future of sewage treatment. First, it has been shown that adequate treatment is largely the result of contact time within the treatment reactors.[217] Contact time is a product of the capacity of the plant and flow rate of the waste stream. This capacity can be exceeded by storm overflows that merge with the sewage plumbing during periods of heavy precipitation and even by excessive water consumption. Important attention must be paid to engineer and maintain a system that is never overloaded. Additional capacity should be promptly added as needed. Insufficiently treated sewage is not much better than simply raw dumping.

Not only a primary (mechanical) and a secondary (decomposition) treatment is necessary.[218] Tertiary treatment is essential to healthy waterways. Tertiary treatment consists of the removal of nitrogen, phosphorous, and chemicals as well as disinfection.[219] While the acute effects that treated wastewater may have on adjacent waterways is often a function of the flow dynamics around the discharge point, eventually all waters merge; relying on currents to carry effluents away is merely another way of sweeping the dirt under the carpet. Disinfection techniques have also been studied closely and the growing consensus is that UV and ozonation strategies are preferable due to the potentially harmful side effects of chlorine-like approaches.[220] UV and ozone treatments are more costly and energy intensive to implement, but are clearly worth the effort in light of the ever increasing load of bacteria, viruses, and other pathogens being found throughout natural systems. Some recent studies are discovering that medicinal and other chemicals in the waste stream are having dangerous effects of surrounding wildlife.[221] The proper handling of manufactured chemicals may be adequately addressed by primary-tertiary[222] treatment or may require specific treatments tailored to individual chemicals.[223] In some cases no effluent standards have ever been set for the chemicals, thereby avoiding treatment altogether.[224] The manufacturers of these chemicals need to be included in the process of devising individualized waste strategies and should also be required to share the additional clean up costs. Once an adequate level of treatment has been achieved, the effluent may be discharged into the receiving waterway or wetland, and the remaining sludge and solids are ready for conversion to useful products.

The preferred treatment modality for sewage solids, due to energy efficiencies, is anaerobic digestion (AD). AD reduces the volume of waste as well as producing three important by-products: biogas (see discussion in Energy), a solid compost material, and a liquid fertilizer. To the extent that a particular locality has good reason for disfavoring the higher AD use, then sludge material and recovered solids can be processed either via Thermal Depolymerization into a crude oil (See Energy), or can be sent to a Plasma Arc facility, or can be reduced to Solid Recovered Fuel, or converted into hydrogen through steam methane reforming, or fed to algae.

Algae cultivation presents one of the most interesting forms of both solid waste nutrient recovery and fossil fuel emissions sequestration. Although the algae oil can be used to produce biofuels, these are then eventually burned, releasing the greenhouse gases all over again (it is important to remember the distinction between CO_2 captured from new emissions versus previously released CO_2 taken directly from the atmosphere; only biofuels created using the latter are renewable and sustainable). A more sustainable use of algae can be found as a human nutritional supplement[225] or as an ingredient in agri- and aqua-cultural fertilizers and feeds. The potential uses of algae as a waste sink are widespread and extremely promising. Equally enticing is the prospect of enhancing more traditional methods of primary and secondary treatment with titanium dioxide treatment (TiO_2). TiO_2 is capable of breaking down toxic and non-toxic organic materials into CO_2 and water using nothing but light energy.[226] Although this process would require CO_2 capture, the anticipated emergence of a CO_2 economy would make this a valuable byproduct.

I dream (please, no snickers) of the self sustaining, comprehensive waste treatment facility of the future that gasifies solid wastes, treats sewage, generates enough electricity to run both the solid waste side and the UV treatment side of the process, while at the same time creating a stream of recycled materials and nutritional supplements, and capturing the bulk of its emitted greenhouse gases. This is not beyond our current technological abilities. What is needed is public education on this often ignored subject and then the funding to implement and sustain infrastructure upgrades. One large source of funding will be the money saved from landfilling, hauling, and sorting activities. Another potential source of funding is the carbon tax and credit system proposed earlier.[227] Under this system, greenhouse gas avoidance through CO_2 capture, becomes a source of income.

A final potential source of funding brings me back to the concept of pay to throw away. By creating a metered system whereby individuals and businesses are charged a fee for waste services based on service consumption, a new stream of revenues will be created. At the same time, a strong incentive to reduce waste production is created. I am speaking of nothing less than charging for waste by the pound, weighed by a new generation of garbage trucks that are able to weigh inputs and keep automated tabs for each address or multiple-dwelling. I realize the logistical complexities of such a measure and can only say that complex problems require complex solutions. With our without garbage metering, the often disregarded problems of solid waste disposal and sewage treatment present a growing global challenge requiring creatively engineered and financed solutions.

FREQUENTLY ASKED QUESTIONS

What is better for the environment, throwing food waste into the trash or down the drain with a food disposal?

That all depends on what types of systems are in place where you live for solid and sewage waste treatment and disposal. In some places, sewage treatment is strained beyond capacity and therefore any additional loading means poorer performance. In places where biomass to energy systems are in place, then the solid waste route is preferable. In places where sewage treatment includes the co-production of biogas, compost, and fertilizers then the drain is preferred. In places with both biomass and sewage by-product programs, the drain is the way to go (due to the co-production of compost and fertilizers from the sewage process). Oil and grease should always go into the trash, unless you have a biodiesel engine to feed.

How can I find out what my locality does with waste?

Most local governments have a sewage and waste department with a web site. These agencies are mandated by law to produce annual reports describing operations and results from the preceding year. These reports should contain all the information needed. These same web sites often contain materials addressing future plans and policies. Most waste and sewage departments also have a community relations officer to help with gathering information about the services provided. Furthermore, individual waste and sewage treatment facilities often have their own websites that explain the operation and provide contact numbers for further information. Local community boards and citizens groups are also good sources of waste treatment information.

Is there anything we can do with existing landfills?

One of the newest waste to energy processes, Plasma Arc Gasification, is being used in Florida to mine an old landfill for waste biomass.[228] This process recovers material from the landfill and then puts this through the plasma arc reactor together with the stream of current waste so that in a few years the landfill will be empty of refuse.

Is there anything we can do with nuclear waste?

Traditional nuclear waste from uranium reactors poses a troubling challenge for several reasons, not the least of which is that it remains radioactive for tens of thousands of years. Some of the most interesting energy research in recent years concerns the use of thorium as a nuclear fuel. Not only does thorium fission produce a waste that is far easier to dispose of, the thorium reactor is able to use uranium waste as a fuel as well. The thorium reactor cleans uranium waste into far less harmful products, allowing us to recycle and sanitize uranium waste. Spent nuclear fuel may also be recycled in closed-end reactors, but this process is considered a weapons proliferation threat since it involves the production of separated plutonium.[229] Besides burial, these are the only options of which I am aware since plasma arc technology cannot gasify the radioactivity out of these materials.

Can I do anything about sewage treatment in other countries?

Short of becoming a sewage treatment engineer or entrepreneur, the best action is targeted charitable giving. In the area of sewage treatment, the United Nations Environment Programme's "Global Programme of Action (GPA) for the Protection of the Marine Environment from Land-Based Activities" is the only intergovernmental program that addresses the interlinkages between freshwater and the coastal environment.[230] This project assesses and advises governments regarding sewage treatment practices as well as other land based activities. A General Trust Fund in support of the implementation of the GPA has been established and is open to financial contributions. These activities are undertaken by the GPA Coördination Office. Projects for GPA implementation by governments are financed by sources such as the Global Environment Facility (GEF). The GEF is funded by member governments so the best way of contributing here is to encourage your national government to give and to get involved in GEF projects. The World Bank and other regional development banks frequently provide low cost financing for water treatment projects (See Water Management FAQs for details).

How does the Federal Government help finance sewage treatment?

The primary mechanism is the Clean Water State Revolving Fund (CWSRF). This program provides loans to help communities repair and replace aging treatment plants and pipes.[231] The CWSRF budget has been slashed by 33 percent since 2003 and by 50 percent since 2004. On March 9, 2007, the U.S. House of Representatives passed the Water Quality Financing Act of 2007 (H.R. 720) to reauthorize the CWSRF at $14 billion over four years (twice the 2004 level).[232] According to the EPA there is a $300 billion gap between what is currently spent and what communities will need over the next 20 years so this is by no means an excessive proposal.[233]

WATER MANAGEMENT AND
AQUACULTURE

As vast as the Earth's water systems are, we have managed to contaminate almost every drop with our waste materials. Plastics have been found on the deep sea beds, our chemicals seep into subterranean groundwater, our vapors mix with water in the atmosphere, and rain laden with chemicals falls on our heads. A large part of everything we discard winds up in some form or another in the Earth's waters. In this light, our discussions about waste, deforestation, and energy are also discussions about water and our actions in those areas will greatly affect the fate of our aqueous assets. These activities though are not the only ones that burden our waters. Human habitation, agricultural irrigation, industrial cooling, hydropower geoengineering, and fishing are also water system stressors. These activities boil down to three main types of impact: habitat destruction, overharvesting, and eutrophication.

Eutrophication is the result of the overfeeding of water borne plants and algae by fertilizers, nutrients, and wastes.[234] Eutrophication can occur naturally, but its frequency and extent has been aggravated considerably by human inputs from agricultural run off and sewage effluents. Just as accelerated climate change is the result of excessive greenhouse gas concentrations in the atmosphere caused by human activities, eutrophication is the result of excessive nitrogen and phosphorous loading into aqueous systems. When nutrients accumulate in watery environments, an explosion of plant growth often follows. As a result of this primary plant production, herbivorous consumers are unable to keep up and a large amount of the plant matter winds up sinking to the bottom. As this material decays, so much oxygen is consumed by the decomposition that anything else trying to survive in these waters winds up asphyxiated for lack of oxygen. These areas are called dead zones and are appearing with increasing frequency in coastal areas around the world.[235] Many people in post-industrialized nations are unaware of how grave a problem coastal zone eutrophication is around the world since it has been drastically eradicated in places where agriculture and sewage treatment are given due attention. Nevertheless, there are still many places where raw sewage is dumped directly into waterways and where agricultural managers pay little attention to the problem of run off. Some recent work by marine biologists in Australia has linked the decline of sections of the Great Barrier Reef to a cascade of events stemming from sugar cane fertilizer run off.[236]

The interface between land and water that forms the coastal or riparian zone is one of the most biologically important on the planet. This area includes submerged land as well as the tidal and wetland zones. The coastal zone is hugely important as a nursery zone for land, water, and amphibian species. It is also an area where a huge proportion of the human population has chosen to live. The confluence of these factors suggests that we need to monitor our habitation patterns and coastal zoning so as not to completely eradicate these habitats for other species. In practice this means creating as much coastal protected area as possible by preventing wide scale human conversion of these zones.[237] In a system where real estate is private property subject to an owner's dominion, this can only mean one thing, protective purchases of coastal land or restrictive easements by conservancies (see FAQs).

We have already touched on the sewage treatment necessary to reduce these excess nutrients from building up. The major source of excess nitrogen and phosphorous however is the agricultural industry. The most promising strategies are those that reduce the irrigation needs of crops (thereby reducing run off and erosion) and those that reduce the fertilizer inputs (thereby reducing the amount of these nutrients that can leach out of the soil). There is a direct relationship between watershed management and eutrophication. A recent study of the Mississippi River Basin, for instance, found that watershed areas with the highest rates of fertilizer runoff had the lowest amount of land enrolled in federal conservation programs.[238]

Plant biotechnology is moving slowly but steadily towards engineering crops that require less water and fertilizer. The question remains whether the new technologies will be developed and transferred to the developing world in time to avoid an irreversible catastrophe. Another of the most interesting strategies is a type of fertilizer made from agricultural wastes called agrichar that drastically improves soil fertility, does not leach out into waterways, and requires very little application.[239] Zero emissions is the goal of closed food production systems such as pond aquaculture and hydroponics. An interesting experimental project along these lines involves the use of deep, desert aquifers in a combined aquaculture and hydroponic agriculture system.[240] This system would open up virtually unlimited food production space, eliminate the need for many pesticides while controlling the diffusion of others, avoid climate based harvest failures, and reduce irrigation requirements for agriculture. The water from the aquaculture process can be used for hydroponics and the agricultural waste, in turn, is added to the fish feedstocks. Desert hydroponics/aquaculture and other forms of hydroponics are still in their infancy but could also someday allow for total control over agricultural impacts, especially if the research is funded at levels commensurate with the severity of the water threats facing us.

We depend on the waters for a large amount of our protein and some of our animal and fish feeds.

An estimated 75% of the world's fisheries are overfished.[241] This number is on the rise.[242] Therefore it should come as no surprise that the tonnage of aquaculture production has also been climbing at a dizzying pace.[243] While, in theory, aquaculture can be viewed as a countermeasure to overfishing, the hard statistics are proving otherwise as both overfishing and aquaculture continue to rise. Furthermore, certain aquacultural production practices, if condoned, threaten to make the entire endeavor a counterproductive one. First, different aquacultured species require varying amounts and types of feed. Carnivorous fish for instance require large amounts of oily fish in their feed; so much so that the net weight balance of fish produced versus fish applied as feed is negative (more fish need to be turned into feed than are eventually harvested for human use).[244] Other types such as Tilapia can be grown inland in closed containers and fed grain or algal feeds.[245] Not only do these herbivorous species reduce pressure on wild feed fish, they can also be grown in zero water exchange enclosures thus eliminating the second major problem, chemical and genetic contamination. Enclosures permit the capture and treatment of fecal waste and other waste byproducts such as uneaten feed, chemicals, and the like before these substances contaminate surrounding waterways.[246] They also reduce the incidence of escaped cultivars and therefore hybridization with wild stocks. Which is all to say that certain species and types of aquaculture are sustainable and even protective of aquatic biodiversity while others are not.[247] Until such time as we are able to culture a particular fish species in a way that produces a net benefit for wild stocks of feeder fish, and does not aggravate nutrient and toxic loads on adjacent wild waters, then that species should remain off the menu.

Aquaculture research is an important field of scientific endeavor these days, especially in major fish eating nations like Japan and Norway. Techniques, feeds, species, medications, and supplements are all being tested with improving results.[248] Nevertheless, many nations are applying aquaculture techniques that are not beneficial to the waterways. We have already spoken about feedstock inefficiencies. Another major issue is the use of coastal zones for caged aquaculture pens such that essential breeding and nurturing wild habitat is converted to a heavily polluting industrial area.[249] These pens are not only a source of waste but also of disease that can spread into adjacent waters. Open ocean aquaculture holds promise for avoiding coastal zone pollution problems and minimizing operating costs, but special attention needs to be given so that the feed balance remains positive and that genetically modified creatures are not able to escape in large numbers and reproduce. One promising pilot program is producing Cobia in large geodesic pens, but I have not seen any data on the feed sustainability of this operation.[250] The mere fact that a seafood product is farmed is no guarantee of environmental sustainability and consumers need to stay aware of the source of origin of aquacultured products as well as wild caught ones (see Frequently Asked Questions).

The final nail in the coffin of the global water system comes from industrial uses such as the hydroelectric damming of rivers and the siphoning of water for industrial cooling purposes. Often viewed as a green source of power, there is growing evidence that large power dams create another equally serious set of problems. First, dams cause serious habitat destruction and biodiversity losses stemming not only from the flooding of previously dry areas, but also by obstructing the movement of water borne species. Perhaps even more distressing is some new research that the large reservoirs created by dams are producing unexpectedly large amounts of greenhouse gases.[251] Add to this the human displacement often created by these projects and you have another case where the solution creates a cascade of harmful consequences. The net effect of these circumstances is that the world's rivers,[252] lakes,[253] mangroves,[254] estuaries,[255] and coral reefs[256] are increasingly imperiled. Although groundwater is a much understudied segment of the water system it appears that there is cause for concern here as well.[257]

Conservation of aquatic ecosystems is woefully underfunded compared to terrestrial systems, evidenced by the amount of aquatic area versus land space under conservation (see Biodiversity). This tendency to ignore water systems stems perhaps from the traditional view of the global water system as being so vast as to be beyond anthropogenic ruination. For whatever reason, water system conservation is in need of a global financing instrument such as carbon emissions trading for the energy sector or pay-to-throw-away in the waste sector. While there are many strategies that can achieve these ends such as voluntary contribution, ecotourism fees, and the like, policy ideas congruent with market forces and a growth driven economy are badly needed. In the U.S., the Environmental Protection Agency recently initiated a water quality trading program, based on a watershed wide approach, that allows the purchase and sale of pollution reductions between water treatment facilities.[258] Other environmentalists such as Professor Steven De Bie propose a system of biodiversity credits, a Herculean task, yet one that merits some further attention.[259] Loosely drawn, an allotment of credits would be auctioned by the international authority based on a given region's biodiversity value. Certain human activities such as sewage effluent emissions, fertilization of agriculture, and others that have an impact on biodiversity would require the possession of sufficient credits. A sewage treatment plant able to produce zero emissions would sell its credits while one that produces high levels of, say, phosphorous, would need to purchase more credits. In the end though, if the difficulties surrounding the Kyoto Protocol are any indication of the efficacy of global regulatory systems, a wiser approach may be an acceleration of what we have now, a dual system consisting of market based or control instruments in developed nations and international development assistance for infrastructure and conservation projects in poorer nations, environmentally prioritized.

FREQUENTLY ASKED QUESTIONS

What can I do to improve agricultural run off practices?

Since agriculture is usually privately owned and operated, there isn't much that the average citizen can do directly to reduce the agricultural run off and erosion that seeps these nutrients into waterways. Government agencies in charge of agricultural practices do try to implement best practices with varying levels of enforcement around the world. Some of the certification agencies are able to monitor whether producers are using sustainable methods.[260] In practice it is very difficult to keep track of the origins of agricultural products.

On the international stage, the Global Environment Facility (GEF) and the World Bank are major actors in the implementation of agricultural water management projects.[261] At present, the GEF has a budget of about $US 3.13B over four years ($US 782M/year) for all of its activities.[262] The World Bank (WB), acting through the International Development Association and the International Bank for Reconstruction and Development, has lent about $US 1.42B per year over the past six years to

Environmental and Natural Resource projects, or about 7.05% of its total disbursements.[263] Between the GEF and the WB, about $US 4.55B per year goes to international assistance for all environmental projects, with water related activities receiving only a portion of that. The President of the World Bank is traditionally from the United States, and the U.S. is the largest donor to the GEF. These two facts should mean that the U.S. electorate could theoretically influence policy at these agencies if their operations were made part of the national political agenda. Individuals can also invest directly in World Bank bonds, which are normally AAA rated and listed as corporate securities under the name International Reconstruction and Development Bank—although these funds would be used only proportionally for environmental projects. These two adjustments, greater commitment by the WB to environmental lending, plus increased funding for the GEF and the WB, are the most direct avenues to global action on water quality issues of all kinds.

On the national stage, the National Campaign for Sustainable Agriculture is a clearinghouse of information and activities.[264] Learn about Federal Farm Bills, about local regulations, and then speak with your representatives about what you have learned. The only way to make any impact on farming practices is through organized political coöperation leading to more farms using organic and environmentally safe methods. Especially if you live in an agricultural area, you need to become familiar with the sustainable agriculture issues.

How can I prevent harmful hydropower?

Hydropower is an energy policy choice. These choices are made at the governmental level so the only way to influence decision making is through political action. That means knowing what candidates think of issues and voting for the ones who will defend the environment. There is very little that we can do to influence energy policy in other countries apart from supporting Non-Governmental Organizations that are working to defend against megadam projects and advocate for sustainable micro-hydro. The lead international NGO on dams is the International Rivers Network.[265] This site is a gateway to local organizations and activities.

How can I have an impact on fisheries and aquaculture?

There are two primary web sites that provide consumer advisories on fish consumption, not only from the point of view of water and fisheries management, but also human safety, issues:

FishWatch (seafood only):
http://www.nmfs.noaa.gov/fishwatch, *last viewed 9/3/07.*

Seafood Watch (all waters):
http://www.mbayaq.org/cr/SeafoodWatch/web/sfw _factsheet.aspx, *last viewed 9/2/07.*

How can I help to preserve coastal zones?

Last but not least, there are important ways of keeping coastal zones from becoming invaded by humans in search of real estate and recreation. Organizations such as the Nature Conservancy[266] actively purchase and preserve wilderness areas all over the world. Find one you like and give according to the formula discussed in biodiversity: one percent of your gross annual income to activities that keep wilderness areas wild. Coastal zones are also vulnerable to waste and agricultural run off creating toxicity and dead zones. These problems require participation in the political decision making process (see Waste FAQs).[267]

HUMAN PROLIFERATION AND CONFLICT

Most of us understand the imperatives of survival, both at the individual and the communal levels. Under life or death conditions, the natural environment suddenly becomes dispensable. Does anyone stop to think how a massive aerial bombardment will affect the biodiversity of the targeted region? How much care was put into avoiding the destruction of ancestral seed banks in Iraq or Afghanistan?[268] Do starving forest dwellers worry about which species will be providing meat for their families? As has oft been observed, concern for the environment is a luxury available only when survival needs are met. To the extent that people feel unsure about their future existence, due to poverty or other reasons, then their natural environments will be at risk. From the other side of the wealth spectrum, unbridled economic growth can also imperil natural environments. The proper relationship between wealth and the environment requires a balancing act where sufficient wealth is grown while, at the same time, wealth is sufficiently distributed to prevent desperate acts of environmental depredation by the more impoverished segments of the population. This relationship holds true at all levels, from local to international.

These two aspects of human economy, growth and distribution, are activities that influence the environment. Anytime we emphasize one at the expense of the other then the table is set for environmental affronts. Unfortunately, our current economic metrics tend to focus on the growth part of the equation. We very carefully and regularly track such things as national growth rates and corporate growth rates, using statistics such as real growth. Real growth incorporates the rate of inflation and seasonal fluctuations to tell us how much wealth was created during a given period. Stated another way, real growth is a good measure of current productivity. Real growth does not convey information about consumption. Gross national income per capita (GNI-pc) tells us how much each person within the group is consuming on average. GNI-pc does not reflect at all on the distribution of this income (that is measured by Gini, see below), but is a good measure of the relative consumption demands on the Earth's resources made by the entire group.

We rarely pay the same level of attention to distributional equity as we do to the growth and income statistics. Growth and income figures are available almost up to the minute, while distribution stats, if available, can often be seven or more years old. Why is this so? I have no easy answer. The standard argument, that emphasizing growth and income over equity is what stimulates productivity and economic success, ignores the environmental threat posed by economic insecurity in large groups of people. Perhaps if one believes TOC1 conditions apply (see Tragedies of the Commons), or that technology can shield us forever from natural resource depletion, then the environmental threat vanishes.[269] This view not only overestimates our technological ability to compensate for fundamental shifts in biogeochemical conditions (i.e., the balance of nature), but also underestimates the resourcefulness and the anger of people deprived of an equitable share of the economic growth. If climate change and biodiversity loss teach us anything it is that our growth and income world view requires an infusion of distributional equity.

Distributional equity is not simply a matter of taking from one pile and putting in the other. Distribution occurs at many levels: among nations, within nations, and within families. A disconnect at any level threatens global security and individual survival to varying degrees. One of the most well respected statistics used for evaluating distributional equity is the Gini Index (named after the mathematician who introduced the concept).[270] The Gini shows the amount of income inequality within a measured population, independent of the size of the population or the territorial extent of the grouping. A finding of 100 would mean one person in the group has all of the income and everyone else zero, while an index result of zero would mean that everyone has the same income. The lower the index result the more distributional equity. In the U.S. this number has been on the rise since 1970 and as of the latest U.N. calculation stands now at 40.8. For purposes of comparison, the Gini for Germany was last calculated at 28.3, for Sweden 25, for India 32.5, for China 44.7, and for Chile 57.1.[271] The world weighted average is 40.5.

I want to be clear that distributional equity is not to be confused with communist ideology. Communism is a system that defines the working class as the primary beneficiary and controller of economic wealth. Distributional equity does not seek to empower one group or class over another, nor does it imply that everyone is entitled to share economic wealth equally. Should corporate executives have a larger slice than the school teachers, should immigrants from one place receive more than those from another? These types of decisions are social choices. The Gini tries to identify disparities between groups without necessarily passing judgment on which people should receive more than others. Nor does a low Gini score always indicate satisfactory levels of equity at finer grains of resolution. The Gini may reveal that there is perfect distributional equity between group A and group B, but further analysis could show that within groups A and B the Gini score is very high. Even in groups registering low Gini scores, there may still be cases of injustice to be addressed. To correct for this possible situation, a more direct reading of poverty is necessary, and for this I suggest using the percentage of the world's extreme poor living within the country (by definition this means anyone earning less than $1/day).[272]

When thinking about wealth, distribution, and poverty, I have always been haunted by a hypothetical economic scenario from an otherwise forgotten lecture. Suppose two brothers each inherit the same amount, say $1,000.00. Brother A has two children and Brother B has ten. The brothers pass their wealth on and now we have two cousins with $500.00 each and ten with $100.00 each. The children of Brother B, looking upon their cousins, complain that they are victims of a distributional inequity. Should we make the two wealthier cousins transfer some of their wealth to the ten impoverished ones? At the heart of this riddle lies the third most important economic statistic (after growth and Gini): the rate of population growth.[273] Uncontrolled population growth frustrates the task of equitable distribution by slicing up the group pie into ever smaller pieces. One often hears good willed people saying that there are too many people being born in this or that place for any attempt at distribution to be effective. The irony is that economists have shown growth accompanied by distribution is a driver of population control. As people become more wealthy and more secure they tend to have fewer offspring.[274] While we need to control the rate of population growth in the less developed nations, we also need to recognize that these countries are populating too fast because of distributional inequities. Nevertheless, is it fair to reward those reproducing uncontrollably with economic gains attained by others as a result of hard work, planning, and management? The answer is no, but never mind that.

Excessive population growth can be just as much of a threat to distribution as making the rich richer and needs to be viewed as an essential ingredient in the global environmental dynamic. To return to the hypothetical, the offspring of Brother B are likely to keep having larger broods and the day will come when the number of B offspring will overwhelm the resources of the entire system. Brother A's offspring cannot therefore simply say: 'too bad, you made your bed, now sleep in it'. Instead the descendants of A need to establish a system of incentives that will modify the reproductive behavior of the B line while still permitting the A line to enjoy the fruits of controlled growth. Returning to our world, economic aid and development assistance needs to be tied to natural population growth benchmarks. Nations should be given the incentive to reduce their natural growth rates by a system that rewards success in this area with greater amounts of aid and development. While compassion for the extremely poor cannot be withheld, deeper gains in quality of life and dignity for these groups must be tied to policies that elicit greater reproductive control.

These four economic plus one demographic statistics, real growth, GNI-pc, Gini, extreme poverty, and rate of population growth can provide a snapshot of environmental performance for any given population. Obviously they are not the only performance measures worth looking at, but for those who are not professional economists they can provide a bird's eye view of the difficult process of adaptation to the expansion of human numbers across the globe. These figures provide a focus for development priorities and political action within and among nations by indicating which major area(s), economic growth, gross income, income distribution, extreme poverty, or population growth requires the most concerted and immediate action.

FREQUENTLY ASKED QUESTIONS

How do I find out about the environmental economics statistics for individual countries?

There are many statistical data sources on the internet such as Nationmaster, or the United Nations Statistics Division, or the CIA's World Factbook, that provide country by country data usually with about a two year lag time. For your convenience here is one set of hyperlinks:

For GNI-pc:
www.nationmaster.com/graph/eco_gro_nat_inc_per cap-gross-national-income-per-capita;

For Gini:
www.nationmaster.com/graph/eco_inc_equ_un_gin_ ind-income-equality-un-gini-index;

For Real Growth:
www.nationmaster.com/graph/eco_gdp_rea_gro_rat economy-gdp-real-growth-rate;

For Extreme Poverty
www.nationmaster.com/graph/eco_pov_sha_of_all_ poo_peo-poverty-share-all-poor-people;

For Population Growth
www.nationmaster.com/graph/peo_pop_gro_ratpeo ple-population-growth-rate

How do I use the environmental economic statistics to evaluate a country?

Let us take the United States as an example. Using some recent Nationmaster statistics, the U.S. has a Population Growth Rate of .91%, a real economic growth rate of 3.4%, a GNI-pc of $33,070 and a Gini Index of 40.8. To put these numbers into context we determine where they place the U.S. in percentile ranking among all of the nations. The population growth rate places the U.S. at number 128 out of 227, or in the 56.38th percentile. When we exclude migration factors and calculate the natural population growth rate, (birth rate–death rate)/10, the rate is even lower at .588%, or in 66.96th percentile. Natural population growth is a more accurate measure since it does not include gains due to immigration. The economic growth rate puts the U.S. in the 68.24th percentile among nations, and the Gini index in the 42.40th percentile. The GNI-pc places the U.S. in the 2.9th percentile. The percentiles indicate the relative position among nations so that for economic growth for instance, 68.24 out of 100 nations have a higher real growth. Only 42.40 of 100 have a higher Gini (remember that a higher Gini means less equity of distribution) and only 3.9 out of a 100 have a higher income. The U.S. is somewhere at the top of the bottom half on population growth, in the lowest third with regard to economic growth, in the top 10% as to consumption (GNI-pc), and in the top half of Gini indices. The data show that the U.S. is below the radar in the extreme poverty scale (meaning that there are negligible numbers of people earning below $1 per day in the U.S.).

The U.S. is a country with a very high level of consumption, a lower than average economic growth rate that nevertheless exceeds its population growth rate (this means that it is experiencing a growth of GNI per capita as well), a more or less average rate of population growth (of which about one third comes from immigration), a lower than average index of distribution equality,[275] and no significant extreme poverty. This suggests that the U.S.'s impact on the environment would be most improved by a lowering of its internal Gini index score and by a reduction in consumption levels. One strategy, although not the only one, would be to distribute some of its real growth to lower income strata of the society via government programs or private donations. If each American (including children) living above the poverty line were somehow able to transfer roughly .5% (half of one percent) of their income per year to those living below the poverty line, then there would be no American living in poverty.

Applying this same methodology to Russia, we have a country that is consuming at a lower than average rate (GNI-pc = $1,764.05, Global Avg = $5,737.28), is showing above average real growth

(6.6%. Global Avg = 5.1%), has a better than average Gini score (39.9, Global Avg = 40.5),[276] is experiencing negative population growth (-.37%), and houses .99% of the world's poorest people. This tells us that the country's economic engine is supplying power and that this power should be applied first to alleviating extreme poverty (which should also improve the Gini), then towards accommodating a larger number of immigrants (which can be viewed as a form of global redistribution of income), and, if desired by the polity, towards raising consumption. I say if desired because the rate of consumption is perhaps a culturally based characteristic and may not be equated with greater levels of happiness by all societies.

This type of information about country dynamics can inform us as to appropriate policies both domestically and internationally. We can then evaluate policies and urge our political representatives to act accordingly.

How do I know if I am donating enough to international charity?

Charity may begin at home but needs also to reach around the world. The world's Gini index is thought to be somewhere around 64 and 66.[277] In order to avoid the global strife and environmental harm that this income disparity will continue to create, nations whose income exceeds the world's mean need to concern themselves with equalizing global distribution. The University of Santa Cruz publishes an impressive set of maps showing various types of global inequality and the degrees of inequality in graphic terms.[278] The U.S.'s high income position (see FAQ 2) means that it must also contribute to equitable distribution on the global scale. Data on official amounts of economic aid are readily available.[279] In the U.S., each person contributes roughly $23.12 per year in official international, economic aid. This puts the U.S. at number 19 of the 22 donor nations. While it is true that this number is probably more than doubled by private and unofficial aid (bringing the figure to perhaps $50.00 per person), these amounts still only raise the U.S.'s standing to about 16. To correct this imbalance, each person in the U.S. should contribute about 2% of their gross income (gross income is the amount called adjusted gross income on Tax Form 1040 plus tax free income not taxed by the 1040) per year to reliable international charities, preferably those that channel their funds to the neediest international cases.[280] While this level of contribution would put us in the number one position among donor countries, it would certainly not resolve the problem of global income inequality. The 2% donation level, if practiced worldwide, would be enough to meet one of the very modest goals of the millenium development project which is to move everyone on Earth above the $1 per day threshold.

FLAWED ECONOMICS

Realizing that we are rapidly losing some of our most precious living resources and perhaps even our own foothold on the planet, I ask who could possibly be against trying to save this? One thread of arguments against taking pro-environmental action derives from the position that environmental protection hurts the economy. Property rights advocates can be heard making statements along the lines of: 'human needs are at the top of the priority list and things like birds and insects are way down the list,' or 'our oil needs take precedence over a herd of caribou.'[281] These statements fall squarely into TOC2 psychology since they recognize a threat to non-human species but give human life a hierarchical priority due to a perceived survival interest (see Tragedies of the Commons). The crux of the problem lies: 1) in the perception that the larger economy will not benefit from environmental protection, and 2) that even if it does benefit, the larger economy will fail to compensate individuals for their private losses resulting from the environmental protection. The first of these concerns is the econometric problem and the second, the distributional problem.

I am not an economist, but if there is one thing I have learned about economic modeling it is that these models tend to suffer from two major flaws: 1) the models are descriptive of the whole, the average, not individuals, and 2) they often omit essential variables. When one uses metrics such as per capita income, it is easy to forget that a datum of 50 could mean that person A's income and person B's income is 50, or that A's is 100 and B's, 0. Is this latter case, where the per capita income is 50, a healthier economy than one with a per capita income of 40, where A's income is 40 and B's, 40? Models built on growth or income alone, omit the variable of equity distribution, and report only total or average results no matter how individual segments of the economy may be faring.

Supposing we have a two sector economy consisting of guns and roses, with a five percent total growth rate. Suddenly someone imposes an environmental policy that makes rose production much more costly but opens the door to a new sector in the economy, fabric flowers. The fabric flower industry replaces much of the rose industry and the overall growth rate increases to six percent (because people like the idea of fabric flowers). Members of the rose industry begin to complain that the economy is going down hill and that environmental protection is killing the economy. This is precisely the effect of environmental protection: disruption in certain segments of the economy, growth in others, and a net positive benefit for the overall economy.[282] Individual responses to environmental protection tend to view the economy from the perspective of one sector, say roses, while the econometrics tell us that the total or average economy is going like gangbusters. Are the individual responses wrong? No, their sector is in decline, but they point the finger at environmental protection when they should be clamoring for a way to participate in the now larger economy.

Still there are those who dispute the overall positive benefit of environmental protection.[283] One position argues that by any standard measure, economic performance is hurt by regulation.[284] This brings us to the important issue of environmental accounting. How we measure economic performance is largely a cultural and social choice that we make based on what we want to use, make, consume, and consider valuable. This is most evident when two cultures meet for the first time and trade according to their internal value systems. In these encounters, shells may be considered as valuable as gold or beads as valuable as large tracts of land. Correspondingly, if we chose to treat environmental qualities as assets, placed a higher demand upon them, and then proceeded to include them in our standards of measurement then we would have a very different picture of how things are and how we should behave economically. Our current economic models place almost no value on a nation's stock of natural assets, be they natural resources or environmental quality. It has always struck me as odd that in business financial accounting, one always keeps track of one's assets, while in national accounting there is no parallel accounting for natural assets. Shouldn't natural assets, their ups and downs, their depreciation, their degradation, also be included in a national accounting just as an inventory of raw materials or the depreciation of a capital asset goes on to the balance sheets of a corporation? Unless and until we include natural assets in our national accounts, the conclusions to be drawn from these models will be flawed and subject to misinterpretation. Instead we will continue to take the environment for granted as something outside of economic decision making, the regulation of which impedes economic performance.

Another argument suggests that in a global economy, raising environmental standards in one place will simply lead to the migration of capital to locations with lower standards, and this argument has empirical support.[285] The underlying problem, the problem of the lowest common denominator determining the rules for everyone, appears in discussions of transboundary pollution, food safety, and product safety. The price of products from nations that set higher environmental standards will be undercut by environmental cheaters. The obvious solution is for the higher standards nation to require its own minimal environmental standards as prerequisites to trade. However, free trade is another one of those economic mantras that often winds up trumping all other considerations. The World Trade Organizations Agreement on Technical Barriers to Trade requires that "all technical standards and regulations must have a legitimate purpose and that the impact or cost of implementing the standard must be proportional to the purpose of the standard," and further, obliges WTO Members "to use international standards or parts of them except where the relevant standards would be ineffective or inappropriate in the national situation."[286] These are difficult evidentiary burdens to carry and could easily discourage the use of stringent environmental sustainability standards when regulating imports. This is a policy conflict requiring attention at the highest levels.

The second major thread of arguments against environmental protection is a variation of the old TOC1 thinking. These thinkers suggest that natural resource scarcity can always be overcome by technological progress and choice shifting.[287] Just as we did with olive oil and then whale blubber, when we begin to run out of petroleum, the argument goes, we will find better extraction methods and more efficient production methods, and then shift gradually in to some other form of energy to keep our lights on at night. If we run out of tuna then we will simply have to shift our preferences for some other fish or even some other form of protein. In the meantime we will also devise some form of global geo-engineering project that will take care of the CO_2 problem. There is large dose of faith, perhaps even hubris, behind this tempting line of reasoning. It both overestimates our powers of ingenuity and underestimates the impact of our expanding interference with the balances of nature. The argument ignores the huge qualitative difference between shifting from gasoline based vehicles to natural gas and changing the temperature of the planet, or between switching the protein source on the menu and eradicating all the large predators of the sea. Even if we could satisfy our needs technologically or by constantly switching preferences, the Earth's natural systems and processes may not be as flexible or amenable to human engineering. There are certain things for which there are no substitutes. Things like the composition of the air we breathe, the hydrological cycle, photosynthesis, the nitrogen cycle, the ozone shield, and many others in this category are simply irreplaceable. These biogeochemical systems, in their current configurations, are essential to our continuing ability to survive on this planet and we need to prevent actions that are likely to interrupt and alter these systems.

There is no doubt that choices made to keep natural systems human-friendly will mean dislocation in certain sectors of the economy. Whaling was once a much larger industry than it is today. When the Singer sewing machine was first introduced, hand sewers everywhere protested that the economy would suffer. What they meant was that their economy would suffer and they were not wrong. In the short run, they would suffer. In the long run though new economies were created and people used their ingenuity to participate in those new economies. The hand sewers learned to use the machines. When someone claims environmentalism will hurt the economy, they are likely referring to a specific sector of the overall economy (probably the one they feel most dependent on for their livelihood) and are usually putting their own interests ahead of the common good. I do not mean to disregard these concerns for they are real and must be included in the mix of policy adjustments. When a fishery is shut down to protect a dwindling stock then those who had been subsisting on that fishery need to be protected. There are many ways to accomplish this end and many accomplished economists who could design the details. One of the best examples of this process comes from the annals of the Nature Conservancy. In 2006, with the aim of reducing the amount of ocean bottom trawling taking place off the coast of California, the Conservancy used its assets to purchase fishing permits and fishing vessels from the fishers.[288] The stock of permits and vessels was then mothballed while the fishers were able to apply their capital resources in other ways. Another example comes from the 110th U.S. Congress, where H.R. 2847, the Green Jobs Act, seeks to provide training for up to 30,000 workers per year in the renewable energy sector.

I am a believer in the capacity of business corporations to respond efficiently to changing business conditions, as long as they are receiving notice of the signals that these conditions are changing. When a government somehow shields the corporation from the news that conditions are changing then we have problems. If we keep bailing out flawed business plans with subsidies or by ignoring the costs of pollution, for example, then we are cooking the books in a way that can seriously hurt an overall economy. Take the U.S. auto industry as an example: by sending signals to this industry that efficiency and pollution were optional design considerations, the wrong message was conveyed, much to the detriment of this industry and all those dependent on it for their livelihoods. In recent years buy outs of the auto workers followed, much the same as for the California fishers, and in both cases because of a misapprehension of environmental factors. Should these auto workers invest their buy out capital into Toyota, then we will have seen, in microcosm, how environmentally oriented decision making transforms economic systems and favors certain producers over others. Companies hoping to survive these transformations need to be sent the message that environmental design, sometimes called cradle to cradle design,[289] is mandatory.

The most important lesson to be learned with respect to business corporations and the environment is that the corporation, as an organizational entity, is second to none in its ability to maximize human ingenuity. To serve this function its industrial intelligence, as it were, must be as accurate and complete as possible. If the larger society fails to communicate to the corporation that, for instance, emissions of a noxious gas are going to cost X amount of dollars, then the corporation is simply going to ignore emissions of the gas. If emissions are understood to trigger a significant cost, then the corporation is going to raise heaven and earth to lower that cost. Recent history, such as the U.S. auto industry example, has shown us that the most inexpensive way for the corporation to avoid that cost is by manipulating the political system to prevent the cost from being imposed altogether—not a healthy relationship for the business corporation in the long run. This arrangement is the equivalent of going to a doctor who will charge only $100 to say everything is fine instead of another who charges only $50 but prescribes $200 worth of medications. If the patient is not sick then the first option is the wiser, otherwise, the second.

Whether patient Earth is sick or not is a question for each of us to study carefully, being that this patient is so important to us and our offspring. I would hope that each and every capable person, once having been informed of the diagnosis, would research the state of the illness, get second opinions, learn the facts, and study the issues with the same amount of effort and concern as when confronted with the grave diagnosis of a loved one. As I can attest, with a little patience and perseverance the fundamentals of environmental science and policy are within the grasp of the average human mind. A growing mountain of evidence concerning biodiversity losses, climate changes, toxic loads, and resource depletions suggests that all is not well and is instead undergoing a rapid decline (by rapid I mean reaching a critical mass within the next 150 years, which is only about three to five generations). It then inevitably follows that society needs to send the environmental message loud and clear to the business corporations confident that they will respond with the awe inspiring effectiveness and creativity that they can deliver. Civil society may send this message via its consensual political representation and by its consumption choices.

FREQUENTLY ASKED QUESTIONS

Is environmental regulation bad for business?

There is no denying that regulation hampers certain business sectors in the short run, but there are other values to consider aside from freedom from regulation. Regulation is a form of communicating from the society at large to a particular sector or sectors of the economy that they need to adapt to new conditions. If they are able to respond as vigorous business corporations should, then the regulation will serve as an impetus for innovation and also market leadership which in the long run is very good for both that business and the economy as a whole.[290]

Can technology counter balance environmental harms forever?

This is undoubtedly a speculative and subjective issue. I personally doubt it. The reason is that the scale of the Earth is much larger than anything we can engineer and the time frames are much longer than we can manage.[291] The current levels of gases, nutrients, energy and ecosystem balances and other natural systems have taken billions of years and enormous amounts of energy to achieve. At the same time we are beginning to appreciate the effects of geometric population growth. In 1700 the estimated global population was about 600 million persons, in 2000 we arrived at about six billion, and a recent UN report projected that global population will peak at 9.2 billion in 2075.[292] After that it will continue to grow, albeit at a slower pace. At the same time economic growth, consumption, waste, democracy, and equality will continue to expand, placing ever greater demands on Earth's systems and human management.

I believe there exists a danger of a coming time in history when humanity becomes a victim of its own success and blind optimism. There will be too many people consuming and making all kinds of waste for the Earth to sustain. When this time arrives, there will be a crash, either from without (disease, malnutrition, etc.) or from within (wars) and population numbers will fall back to a level that is sustainable. We may be seeing early and relatively small scale evidence of this today with our almost constant state of war amongst ourselves and against infectious and environmental diseases. This paradox is at the core of the environmental enigma. The more successful we become at dominating our world the closer we are to overburdening the Earth's systems with catastrophic consequences. This will be a never ending process unless we can figure out ways of lessening our burden on natural services and resources.

This too will require our technological skills, but with a new orientation. I believe this is possible, but only if we make this a fundamental aspiration for all humanity, as important as freedom, justice, or equality. Every corner of the Earth needs to adopt wholeheartedly the principles of the new environmental economy and turn these principles into enforceable foundations of the world's legal and political systems.

What can I do to make the business world more responsive to environmental imperatives?

The business world tends to respond to economic cues more than popular opinion. The most effective measure is to spend money on the products and investments that are congruent with forward thinking environmental ideas. Making such a determination can be difficult in practice and the availability of such information can vary widely between industries. A good place to start is the U.S. EPA's Green Power Partners List.[293] This is a growing group of companies that are partnering with the EPA to maximize their energy efficiency. An even more select and committed group receives the annual Green Power Leadership Award. Showing a preference for these companies as both a consumer and an investor will send a message. When purchasing a product, pay attention to whether it is eco-labeled. Since there are a variety of labeling organizations, become familiar with their criteria at the Consumer Union's Guide.[294] You may also use this site as a source of information on specific products that are currently certified. There is a learning curve associated with making environmentally conscious decisions but the goal makes the effort worthwhile, and as the business community becomes more and more receptive to the message, the information gathering should become less of a burden. Finally, don't be shy about telling your vendors to offer products that are eco-labeled.

AFTERWORD:
The Age of Preventropy

I began this essay by stating that the last hundred or two years of world history have seen the emergence of what I call a TOC2 state (see Tragedies of the Commons), and that insofar as humanity resists this TOC2 world view, then a Ecocidal Age with potentially devastating consequences is bound to perdure. My struggle with these environmental demons has shown me that lifelines are in sight. An awesome amount of environmental data, support services, research, and technology is available for the taking, and all we have to do is to use these tools to inform today's decisions. What will that take? Leadership, money, and political will are the obvious answers, but what underlies these factors is more fundamental. As I hinted earlier, the TOC2 shift could have implications as profound as the passage from hunting and gathering to agriculture or the emergence of the scientific method during the Renaissance. The TOC2 shift in world view would allow humanity to pass through the Age of Ecocide into a new age. I caught an inkling of this new world view in the concept of negative entropy, or negentropy, first introduced by the ideas of Erwin Schrödinger,[295] and Nicholas Georgescu-Roegen,[296] and later refined by many other theorists.[297] I am persuaded by my research that we live in the dawn of the Age of Preventropy.

Most students of physics will remember that entropy is "a natural tendency of all matter and energy in the universe to evolve towards a state of inert uniformity."[298] The concept was introduced in 1850 by Rudolf Clausius, whose classic example involved the melting of ice in a glass of water.[299] Since every process results in an overall increase in entropy and a corresponding degradation in energy,[300] energy from the Sun undergoes some entropy on the way here, and then some more as it passes through the plant world and then the animal world, and into the fossil fuels we then burn. Along the way, the energy is used by biological systems to propagate life. Eventually all that energy dissipates into such a state of disorder that is becomes nothing, unusable forever. Entropy is also a measure of the loss of information in a transmitted message.[301] What I have been discussing in this book is humanity's impact on the natural progression of entropy. Negentropy, is a force that opposes entropy and seeks to maintain a predictable, steady state within a system.[302] The various policies, techniques, and technologies mentioned throughout this essay are manifestations of, and attempts to harness, negentropy, for the benefit of humankind. Since entropy cannot truly be negated, only delayed, I call this activity preventropy.

The action of entropy on Earth is being catalyzed and accelerated by an increasingly dominant human exploitation of the natural order. Heretofore terrestrial entropy had been minimized by a complex cascade of utilization, recycling, and storage of the Sun's energy into genomes, fossil fuels, and other natural systems. Whenever a species becomes extinct or a natural resource is depleted, in effect, we are witnessing a progression of entropy from one state to a less organized state, either in the sense of energy degradation or of genetic information loss, or both. What characterizes the incipient Age of Preventropy is humanity's self-awareness and reaction to this state of accelerated entropy. It comes from the realization that the human species depends on <u>the prolongation of a specific entropic state, one that is hospitable to our physiological needs.</u> The consequences of this realization are profound and affect everything from technological development to political theory to dietary choices to modes of transportation to recreational activities. Social transformations of this magnitude do not occur overnight and results will not appear in an instant. The kernel of the process is psychological adjustment, followed by as much concrete, scientifically informed action as incremental progress will allow.

It has been my strategy of late to make small changes in my life consistent with this new found knowledge.[303] The last thing from my mind has been to give up on the quality of life I enjoy, purchased by the blood, sweat, and tears of countless forbears. I am not a Luddite, nor a believer in the banana principle (= build absolutely nothing anywhere near anyone), or getting off the grid, or reverting to a life without toys, comforts, bells and whistles. The purpose of the program is to reorient, to consider each action in accordance with the principle of preventropy. The transformation will raise our of quality of life to a level that can be enjoyed by as many people as possible for as long as the eye can see. We need to use technology even more, to bring more people out of poverty, to have more freedom, to reward effort with prosperity, to have more recreational time, to live longer lives, to travel the globe, to throw out the trash without thinking twice, to encounter strange cultures and wild creatures, to eliminate the need for wars, and to enjoy the pleasures of life. The insight of this book should be that all these human aspirations are rooted in environmental science and policy.

If there is one final precautionary word to remember it should be hysteresis. Hysteresis is the "lagging of an effect behind its cause."[304] The biodiversity losses and climate change effects we are witnessing on Earth today are a form of hysteresis, lagging behind many, long term causes. We can also expect a sizeable delay before any remedial actions we take today show any effect. As an example consider that although there has been a ban against ozone depleting chemicals for many years, in 2006 the Antarctic ozone hole remained larger than ever.[305]

We cannot be sure that preventative actions will have their desired effect since the biogeochemical changes on Earth could already be irreversible or unstoppable. Nevertheless, the concept of hysteresis warns that if we wait for irrefutable proof that the terrestrial Humpty Dumpty is in fact about to fall, then we will have run out of time. Only if we each begin taking action now, and with a great deal of luck, will we be able to keep our wobbly world from taking a tumble against our most exalted interests. Whether or not we succeed, my own experience has shown that making the switch to a preventropy based view of the world produces a spiritual rebirth. I have never felt like a freer, more connected person than I do today.

New York, New York
December 06, 2008

EPILOGUE:
International Ecocide Law

This epilogue is being written in May of 2017. The last several years have seen the uprising of a movement to make Ecocide a crime before the International Criminal Court (ICC). I have collaborated on this effort by chairing a committee tasked with the drafting of the enacting amendments to the International Court Statute. By means of the NGO End Ecocide on Earth, the amendments are being promoted and advocated before the United Nations as well as the 124 nation-states who are parties to the ICC so that the ecocide law may be considered for adoption at an upcoming Assembly of the Parties. The full set of amendments may be viewed here: http://image.xyxy.info/AmendICC.pdf .

ABOUT THE AUTHOR

Adam D. Carfagno Cherson is an International Ecological Policy Attorney. From 2006 until 2015 he edited *Ecosider* (ecosider.wordpress.com). In 2006, he co-authored the white paper "Addressing Electronic Waste in New York City" for the Natural Resources Defense Council. His book review of "An Ocean Blueprint for the 21st Century" appeared in Columbia's Journal of International Affairs in 2005. From 2006 to 2007 he was a member of the International Environmental Law Committee of the Association of the Bar of the City of New York. In 2007, he was a member of the Reef Educational Foundation scuba team that surveyed the Flower Garden Banks in the Gulf of Mexico as part of a NOAA expedition to the area. His article *"Rapid Site Selection and Performance Measurement of Marine Reserves...,"* published on Reefbase.org, applies GIS modeling and Landsat satellite imagery to the largest known database of Caribbean fish species sightings. He is a photographic contributor to Fishbase.org, an international ichthyological database developed by the World Fish Center and the Food and Agriculture Organization of the United Nations. He holds an AB from Harvard University, a JD from Tulane Law School, and an MPA in Environmental Science and Policy from Columbia University.

ENDNOTES

[1] Some examples of these programs include: Project BudBurst (http://www.windows.ucar.edu/citizen_science/budburst/); The Encyclopedia of Life (http://www.eol.org/index); World Water Monitoring Day (http://www.worldwatermonitoringday.org/); and Reef Foundation (http://www.reef.org/programs /volunteersurvey).

[2] See Rapanos v. US, 547 US 715 (2006); http://supreme.justia.com/us/547/04-1034/

[3] Hartig, E.K., et al. 2002. Anthropogenic and Climate Change Impacts on Salt Marshes of Jamaica Bay, New York City. Wetlands. 22(1): 71-89.

[4] Hartig, E.K., et al. 2002. Anthropogenic and Climate Change Impacts on Salt Marshes of Jamaica Bay, New York City. Wetlands. 22(1): 71-89.

[5] Hartig, E.K., et al. 2002. Anthropogenic and Climate Change Impacts on Salt Marshes of Jamaica Bay, New York City. Wetlands. 22(1): 71-89.

[6] Bertness, M.D., Ewanchuk, P.J., and Silliman, B.R. 2002. Anthropogenic modification of a New England Salt marsh landscape. PNAS. 99(3): 1395-1398.

[7] Bertness, M.D., Ewanchuk, P.J., and Silliman, B.R. 2002. Anthropogenic modification of a New England Salt marsh landscape. PNAS. 99(3): 1395-1398.

[8] Bertness, M.D., Ewanchuk, P.J., and Silliman, B.R. 2002.

Anthropogenic modification of a New England Salt marsh landscape. PNAS. 99(3): 1395-1398.

[9] Hartig, E.K., et al. 2002. Anthropogenic and Climate Change Impacts on Salt Marshes of Jamaica Bay, New York City. Wetlands. 22(1): 71-89.

[10] Steinberg, N., et al. 2004. Health of the Harbor: The First Comprehensive Look at the State of the NY/NJ Harbor Estuary. A report to the NY/NJ Harbor Estuary Program. Hudson River Foundation: New York, NY.

[11] Bertness, M.D., Ewanchuk, P.J., and Silliman, B.R. 2002. Anthropogenic modification of a New England Salt marsh landscape. PNAS. 99(3): 1395-1398.

[12] Silliman, B.R., and Bertness, M.D. 2002. A Trophic Cascade Regulates Salt Marsh Primary Production. PNAS. 99(16): 10500-10505.

[13] Hartig, E.K., et al. 2002. Anthropogenic and Climate Change Impacts on Salt Marshes of Jamaica Bay, New York City. Wetlands. 22(1): 71-89.

[14] Hartig, E.K., et al. 2002. Anthropogenic and Climate Change Impacts on Salt Marshes of Jamaica Bay, New York City. Wetlands. 22(1): 71-89.

[15] Feinberg, J.A., and Burke, R.L. 2003. Nesting Ecology and Predation of Diamondback Terrapins, Malaclemys terrapin, at Gateway National Recreation Area, New York. Journal of Herpetology. 37(3): 517-526.

[16] Lawrence Page, "Planetary Biodiversity Inventories," ActionBioscience,

http://www.actionbioscience.org/biodiversity/
page.html , *last viewed 9/1/07*; see also: Planetary Biodiversity
Inventories http://www.nsf.gov/news/news_summ.jsp?
cntn_id=103065 , *last viewed 8/18/07*; Census of Marine Life
http://www.thew2o.net/census.html , *last viewed 8/18/07*;
Svalbard Global Seed Vault http://www.croptrust.org/
main/arctic.php?itemid=211 , *last viewed 8/18/07*.

[17] Douglas Allchin, "Error and the Nature of Science,"
ActionBioscience, http://actionbioscience.org/education/
allchin2.html, *last viewed 9/2/07*.

[18] Charlie Rose, "E.O. Wilson and James Watson on Charles
Darwin," December 14, 2005, http://video.google.com/
videoplay?docid=-927851714963534233 *last viewed 8/18/07*.

[19] Niles Eldredge, "The Sixth Extinction," ActionBioscience,
http://www.actionbioscience.org/newfrontiers/eldredge2.html ,
last viewed 9/2/07.

[20] American Museum of Natural History, "Mass Extinction,"
http://www.amnh.org/science/biodiversity/extinction/IntroBa
sicsOngFS.html , *last viewed 9/2/07*.

[21] John Baez, "Extinction," University of California, Riverside,
http://math.ucr.edu/home/baez/ extinction , *last viewed
8/18/07*.

[22] Niles Eldredge, "The Sixth Extinction," ActionBioscience,

 http://www.actionbioscience.org/newfrontiers/eldredge2.html
, *last viewed 9/2/07*.

[23] ReefQuest Centre for Shark Research, "Biology of Sharks and
Rays-Shark Evolution," http://www.elasmoresearch.org/

education/evolution/geologic_time.htm, *last viewed 8/18/07.*

[24] *The Columbia Encyclopedia*, Sixth Edition, "Turtle,"
http://www.bartleby.com/65/tu/turtle.html , *last viewed 8/18/07.*

[25] V.V. Zerikhin, "Ecological History of the Terrestrial Insects,"
Paleontological Institute of Moscow,
http://palaeoentomolog.ru/
New/ecology.html , *last viewed 8/18/07.*

[26] Troy Holder, "Age of Homo Sapiens," The Physics Factbook,
http://hypertextbook.com/facts/1997/TroyHolder.shtml , *last viewed 8/18/07.*

[27] Public Broadcasting Service, "Mystery of the Black Death,"
http://www.pbs.org/wnet/secrets/case_plague/clues.html , *last viewed 8/18/07.*

[28] See: Sharon Moalem, "Survival of the Sickest,"
http://www.survivalofthesickestthebook.com , *last viewed 8/18/07.*

[29] Brian Sykes, *The Seven Daughters of Eve* (New York: W.W. Norton & Co., 2001).

[30] See: Jared Diamond, *Collapse: How Societies Choose to Fail* (Middlesex: Penguin Books, 2005).

[31] Felix Forest, *et al.*, "Preserving the Evolutionary Potential of Floras in Biodiversity Hotspots," *Nature* 2007, 445: 757–760.

[32] Brian Sykes, *The Seven Daughters of Eve* (New York: W.W. Norton & Co., 2001).

[33] Steve Olson, *Mapping Human History* (New York: Houghton Mifflin, 2003).

[34] Convention on Biological Diversity, "Home Page," Secretariat of the Convention on Biological Diversity, http://www.cbd.int/default.shtml , *last viewed 8/20/07.*

[35] Michael A. Gollin, "Biopiracy: The Legal Perspective," ActionBioscience, http://www.actionbioscience.org/biodiversity/gollin.html , *last viewed 9/1/07.*

[36] Larry Rohter, "As Brazil Defends Its Bounty, Rules Ensnare Scientists," *The New York Times*, August 28, 2007, electronic edition, http://www.nytimes.com, *last viewed 8/28/07.*

[37] Jane Lubchenco *et al.*, "Plugging a Hole in the Ocean: The Emerging Science of Marine Reserves," 2003 *Ecological Applications*, 13(1):S3–S7.

[38] See: Catherine Rich and Travis Longacre, eds., *The Ecological Consequences of Artificial Night Lighting* (Washington, D.C.: Island Press, 2005); see also: http://www.darksky.org/resources/links/ abstracts.html, *last viewed 8/21/07.*

[39] This figure has been adjusted for inflation into 2006 dollars.

[40] Norman Myers *et al.*, "Biodiversity Hotspots for Conservation Priorities," *Nature* 2000, 403:853–858; see also Alexander James *et al.*, "Balancing the Earth's Accounts," 1999 *Nature*, 401:323–324.

[41] World Bank, "2007WorldDevelopmentIndicators-

4:Economy,"
http://siteresources.worldbank.org/DATASTATISTICS/Resou
rces/WDI07section4-intro.pdf , *last viewed 8/20/07.*

[42] Jason D. Fridley *et al.*, "Genetic Identity of Interspecific
Neighbors Mediates Plant Responses to Competition and
Environmental Variation in a Species-rich Grassland," *Journal of
Ecology* 2007, 95(5): 908–915.

[43] Global Environment Facility, "Projects,"
http://www.gefweb.org/projects/Focal_Areas/focal_areas.html
, *last viewed 8/30/07.*

[44] Convention on International Trade in Endangered Species of
Wild Fauna and Flora, "The CITES Species,"
http://www.cites.org/eng/disc/species.shtml , *last viewed
8/20/07.*

[45] Scientific Certification Systems, "Home Page,"
http://www.scscertified.com , *last viewed 8/20/07*

[46] National Marine Fisheries Service, " FishWatch," National
Oceanographic and Atmospheric Administration,
http://www.nmfs.noaa.gov/fishwatch , *last viewed 8/20/07.*

[47] Rainforest Alliance, "Shop Certified,"
http://ra.eximware.net/RA , *last viewed 8/20/07*

[48] Mongabay, "Deforestation Figures for Selected Countries,"
http://rainforests.mongabay.com/deforestation , *last viewed
8/20/07.*

[49] See e.g., Eco-Labels, "The Consumer Union's Guide to
Environmental Labels," http://www.eco-labels.org/home.cfm ,
last viewed 8/20/07.

[50] Socioeconomic Data and Applications Center, "Pilot 2006 Environmental Performance Index," U.S. National Aeronautics and Space Administration, http://sedac.ciesin.columbia.edu/es/ epi/downloads.html , *last viewed 8/20/07.*

[51] World Commission on Protected Areas, "World Database on Protected Areas," http://www.unep-wcmc.org/wdpa , *last viewed 8/20/07.*

[52] Intergovernmental Panel on Climate Change, "Home Page," United Nations, http://www.ipcc.ch , *last viewed 8/20/07.*

[53] For a general introduction to abiotic climate change, see S. George Philander, Is the Temperature Rising? (Princeton: Princeton University Press, 1998).

[54] U.S. Environmental Protection Agency, "Atmosphere Changes," http://epa.gov/climatechange/science/recentac.html , *last viewed 9/3/07.*

[55] Some of the journals covering this topic include *Global Change Biology*, *Global Environmental Change*, and *Nature Reports: Climate Change.*

[56] The extent of arctic sea ice, for instance, is reaching an all time low: National Snow and Ice Data Center, "Home Page," University of Colorado, http://www.nsidc.org , *last viewed 08/21/07.*

[57] Intergovernmental Panel on Climate Change, "Home Page," United Nations, http://www.ipcc.ch , *last viewed 8/20/07.*

[58] Intergovernmental Panel on Climate Change, "Home Page," United Nations, http://www.ipcc.ch , *last viewed 8/20/07.*

[59] Intergovernmental Panel on Climate Change, "Home Page," United Nations, http://www.ipcc.ch , *last viewed 8/20/07.*

[60] United Nations Framework Convention on Climate Change, " Kyoto Protocol," http://unfccc.int/resource/docs/convkp/kpeng.html , *last viewed 8/20/07.*

[61] A short list of institutions that have declared abiotic global warming is occurring rapidly would include: National Academy of Sciences (NAS), National Oceanic and Atmospheric Administration (NOAA), NASA's Goddard Institute of Space Studies (GISS), Environmental Protection Agency (EPA), The Royal Society of the UK (RS), Canadian Meteorological and Oceanographic Society (CMOS), and the Intergovernmental Panel on Climate Change (IPCC), Larry West, "Is Global Warming a Hoax?," About.com, http://environment.about.com/od/faqglobalwarming/f/gw_fa q_hoax.htm?nl=1 , *last viewed 8/25/07.*

[62] Yale School of Forestry & Environmental Studies, "American Opinions on Global Warming," Yale University, Gallup, and ClearVision Institute Poll 2007, http://environment.yale.edu/ news/5305-americanopinions-on-global-warming/ , *last viewed 11/05/07;* Woods Institute for the Environment at Stanford University, "Second Annual 'America's Report Card on the Environment' Survey," Woods Institute and AP Poll 2007, http://woods.stanford.edu/docs/surveys/GW_200709_AP_sur vey.pdf , *last viewed 11/05/07.*

[63] ClimateCrisis.net, "Calculate Your Impact,"

http://www.climatecrisis.net/takeaction/carboncalculator , *last viewed 08/21/07.*

[64] U.S. Environmental Protection Agency, "Green Power Locator," http://www.epa.gov/greenpower/locator/index.htm , *last viewed 08/21/07.*

54 U.S. Department of Energy, "Energy Savers," http://www.energysavers.gov , *last viewed 08/21/07.*

[65] U.S. Department of Energy, "Energy Savers," http://www.energysavers.gov , *last viewed 08/21/07.*

[66] Clean Energy Partnership, "Home Page," http://www.cleanenergypartnership.org , *last viewed 9/3/07;* Clean Air Conservancy, "NETZERO Emissions Calculators," http://www.cleanairconservancy.org/calculator.php , *last viewed 8/30/07.*

[67] See for example: Chicago Climate Exchange, "Home Page," http://www.chicagoclimatex.com/index.jsf , *last viewed 9/2/07.*

[68] The City of New York, "PlaNYC," http://www.nyc.gov/html/planyc2030/ html/plan/plan.shtml, *last viewed 11/02/07.*

[69] EPA, "Personal Emissions Calculator Assumptions and References," http://www.epa.gov/climatechange/emissions/ind_assumptions.html, *last viewed 11/02/07.*

[70] Bjorn Lomborg, *The Skeptical Environmentalist* (Cambridge: Cambridge University Press, 2004, 12 Edition), pp. 259-324.

[71] Bjorn Lomborg, *The Skeptical Environmentalist* (Cambridge:

Cambridge University Press, 2004, 12 Edition), pp. 259-324.

[72] Bjorn Lomborg, *The Skeptical Environmentalist* (Cambridge: Cambridge University Press, 2004, 12 Edition), pp. 259-324.

[73] Bjorn Lomborg, *The Skeptical Environmentalist* (Cambridge: Cambridge University Press, 2004, 12 Edition), pp. 259-324.

[74] Bjorn Lomborg, *The Skeptical Environmentalist* (Cambridge: Cambridge University Press, 2004, 12 Edition), pp. 259-324.

[75] Garret Hardin, "The Tragedy of the Commons," *Science, New Series* 1968, 3859: 1243–1248.

[76] It is conceivable for a eutopian to adopt a TOC1 view of the environment. In that case the desire to share with future generations is motivated not by a perceived resource scarcity, but by such factors as ethical norms, social traditions, political compromise, or mere precaution.

[77] Calculated using data provided by Global Footprint Network, http://www.footprintnetwork.org/download.php?id=305 , *last viewed 08/18/2007.*

[78] Advocates of this concept include Glenn Hubbard, Alan Greenspan, Sam Nunn, Pete Domenici, Robert Frank and Warren Buffet, to name a few; see *e.g.*: "Buffet on 'Progressive Consumption Tax'," MSN Video, http://video.msn.com/?mkt=en-us&fg=rss&vid=07c3d75bb448-48ba-883a-59fb0d699a8c&from=34 , *last viewed 11/03/07.*

[79] See: Thomas C. Schelling, *Micromotives and Macrobehavior*, (New York: W.W. Norton, Revised Edition, 2006).

[80] National Renewable Energy Laboratory, "Home Page," http://www.nrel.gov , last viewed 9/01/07; U.S. Department of Energy, "Home Page," http://www.doe.gov , *last viewed 9/01/07.*

[81] U.S. Department of Energy, "Grid 2030," http://www.energetics.com/pdfs/electric_power/electric_visio n.pdf , *last viewed 8/30/07.*

[82] Network for New Energy Choices, "Freeing the Grid," www.newenergychoices.org/uploads/netMetering.pdf , *last viewed 8/31/07*; Rosanne Skirble, "Consumers Generate Cleaner Energy Future," Voice of America, January 29, 2007, http://www.voanews.com/english/archive/2007-01/2007-01-18-voa69.cfm?CFID=120725701&CFTOKEN=97569547 , *last viewed 8/30/07.*

[83] Xiaoying Yang and Benedykt Dziegielewski, "Water Use By Thermoelectric Power Plants in the United States," http://www.blackwell-synergy.com/doi/full/10.1111/j.1752-1688.2007.00013.x , *last viewed 8/31/07.*

[84] MIT Interdisciplinary Panel, "The Future of Coal," 2007, http://web.mit.edu/coal , *last viewed 8/23/07.*

[85] MIT Interdisciplinary Panel, "The Future of Coal," 2007, http://web.mit.edu/coal , *last viewed 8/23/07.*

[86] The FutureGen Alliance, a non-profit organization, represents some of the world's largest coal companies and electric utilities including: American Electric Power, Anglo American, BHP Billiton, the China Huaneng Group, CONSOL Energy Inc., E. ON U.S., Foundation Coal, PPL Corporation, Rio Tinto Energy America, Peabody Energy, Southern Company, and Xstrata

Coal. These companies provide energy to tens of millions of residential, business, and industrial customers in North America, Asia, Australia, Europe, Africa and South America. The Alliance is partnering with the U.S. Department of Energy to design and build the facility. Learn more about FutureGen and the Alliance at www.FutureGenAlliance.org. Since the first edition, the FutureGen Alliance was disbanded by the Bush Administration in 2007-8 and is now being considered for a revival by the Obama Administration.

[87] U.S. Department of Energy, "National Coal Council: Remarks Prepared for Secretary Bodman," http://www.energy.gov/news/4496.htm , *last viewed 8/31/07.*

[88] Kurt Zenz House, *et al.*, "Permanent Carbon Dioxide Storage in Deep Sea Sediments," *Proceedings of the National Academy of Sciences*, electronic edition, August 7, 2006, http://dx.doi.org/10.1073/pnas.0605318103 , *last viewed 8/31/07.*

[89] PhysOrg, "Ohio CO_2 Sequestration Test Well Completed," http://www.physorg.com/news96655006.html , *last viewed 8/31/07.*

[90] PhysOrg, "Chemists Design World's Lowest Density Crystals For Use in Clean Energy," http://www.physorg.com/news95617436.html , *last viewed 8/31/07.*

[91] Turid Synnøve Aas *et al.*, "Feed Intake, Growth and Nutrient Utilization in Atlantic Halibut (*Hippoglossus hippoglossus*) Fed Diets Containing a Bacterial Protein Meal," *Aquaculture Research* 2007, 38(4): 351–360, http://dx.doi.org/10.1111/j.1365-2109.2007.01672.x , *last viewed 8/25/07.*

[92] PhysOrg, "Students Develop New Ways to Produce Renewable Fuels,"
http://www.physorg.com/news97778376.html , *last viewed 8/31/07.*

[93] Amy Feldman, "Skyscraper Farms," *Popular Science*, July 2007, electronic edition,
http://www.popsci.com/popsci/environment/f2105a914b6b31 10vgnvcm1000004eecbccdrcrd.html , *last viewed 8/26/07.*

[94] Science Daily, "Device Uses Solar Energy To Convert Carbon Dioxide Into Fuel,"
www.sciencedaily.com/releases/2007/04/070418091932.htm , *last viewed 8/31/07.*

[95] The Geological Society of America, "The Geology and Climatology of Yucca Mountain and Vicinity, Southern Nevada and California,"
http://rock.geosociety.org/Bookstore/default.asp?oID=0&catI D=8&pID=MWR199 , *last viewed 8/31/07.*

[96] MIT Interdisciplinary Panel, "The Future of Nuclear Power," 2003, http://web.mit.edu/nuclearpower , *lastviewed 8/23/07.*

[97] Seth Fletcher, "Nuking Nuclear Waste," Popular Science, electronic edition, April 2007,
http://www.popsci.com/popsci/science/691f6912e3022110vgn vcm1000004eecbccdrcrd.html , *last viewed 8/31/07.*

[98] Federation of American Scientists, "Plutonium Production," http://www.fas.org/nuke/intro/nuke/ plutonium.htm , *last viewed 8/23/07.*

[99] Australian Uranium Association, "Plutonium: Nuclear Issues

Briefing Paper 18," 2007, http://www.uic.com.au/nip18.htm , *last viewed 8/23/07.*

[100] MIT Interdisciplinary Panel, "The Future of Nuclear Power," 2003, http://web.mit.edu/nuclearpower , *last viewed 8/23/07.*

[101] MIT Interdisciplinary Panel, "The Future of Nuclear Power," 2003, http://web.mit.edu/nuclearpower , *last viewed 8/23/07.*

[102] World Nuclear Association, "Thorium," http://www.world-nuclear.org/info/inf62.html, *last viewed 8/31/07.*

[103] International Atomic Energy Agency, "Thorium Fuel Cycle-Potential Benefits and Challenges," http://wwwpub.iaea.org/MTCD/publications/PDF/TE_1450_web.pdf , *last viewed 8/31/07.*

[104] Tim Dean, "New Age Nuclear," 2006, *Cosmos,* http://www.cosmosmagazine.com/node/348 , *last viewed 8/24/07.*

[105] World Nuclear Association, "Thorium," http://www.world-nuclear.org/info/inf62.html, *last viewed 8/31/07.*

[106] ITER, "Home Page," http://www.iter.org , *last viewed 8/31/07.*

[107] Mark Williams, "Mining the Moon," *Technology Review,* August 23, 2007, electronic edition, http://www.technologyreview.com/Energy/19296/ , *last viewed 8/28/07.*

[108] US Department of Energy, Office of Energy Efficiency and Renewable Energy, "Report to Congress on Renewable Energy Resource Assessment Information for the United States," US

Department of Energy, (October 2006),

http://www.eere.energy.gov/ba/pba/km_portal/docs/pdf/fy06
_epact_201_report.pdf , *last viewed 8/24/07.*

[109] US Department of Energy, Office of Energy Efficiency and Renewable Energy, "Report to Congress on Renewable Energy Resource Assessment Information for the United States," US Department of Energy, (October 2006),

http://www.eere.energy.gov/ba/pba/km_portal/docs/pdf/fy06
_epact_201_report.pdf , *last viewed 8/24/07.*

[110] Iol.co.za, "Hydropower Contributes to Global Warming," http://www.iol.co.za/index.php?set_id=14&click_id=143&art_i d=qw1165558865413S360 , *last viewed 8/23/07.*

[111] Science Daily, "Biology Professor Helps Others Go With the Flow of Dam Removal," http://www.sciencedaily.com/releases/2007/03/070302171346. htm , *last viewed 8/23/07.*

[112] Microhydropower, "Home Page," http://microhydropower.net , *last viewed 8/29/07.*

[113] Peter Fairley, "Tidal Turbans Help Light Up Manhattan," Technology Review, electronic edition, April 23, 2007, http://www.technologyreview.com/Energy/18567 , *last viewed 9/1/07.*

[114] Marine Current Turbines, "Installation of the World's First Commercial Tidal Current Power System Confirmed," http://www.marineturbines.com/mct_text_files/070606.pdf , *last viewed 8/23/07.*

[115] Testimony of Ann F. Miles, Director, Division of Hydropower Licensing, Federal Energy Regulatory Commission, Before the Subcommittee on Fisheries,

Wildlife and Oceans and the Subcommittee on Energy and Mineral Resources Committee on Natural Resources U.S. House of Representatives Hearing on Renewable Energy Opportunities and Issues on the Outer Continental Shelf, April 24, 2007.

[116] US Department of Energy, Office of Energy Efficiency and Renewable Energy, "Report to Congress on Renewable Energy Resource Assessment Information for the United States," US Department of Energy, (October 2006), http://www.eere.energy.gov/ba/pba/km_portal/docs/pdf/fy06_epact_201_report.pdf , *last viewed 8/24/07.*

[117] *Reuters News Service*, "US Wind Power to Grow 26 Percent in 2007," January 24, 2007, Planet Ark, www.planetark.com/dailynewsstory.cfm/newsid/39984/story.htm , *last viewed 8/24/07.*

[118] National Renewable Energy Laboratory, "Wind Research," National Renewable Energy Laboratory, http://www.nrel.gov/wind , *last viewed 8/24/07.*

[119] Matthew Wald, "It's Free, Plentiful and Fickle," *The New York Times*, December 28, 2006, electronic edition, http://www.nytimes.com , *last viewed 12/28/06.*

[120] National Renewable Energy Laboratory, " NREL Newsroom," National Renewable Energy Laboratory, http://www.nrel.gov/news/press/2006/435.html , *last viewed 8/24/07.*

[121] National Renewable Energy Laboratory, "Wind Research,"

National Renewable Energy Laboratory, http://www.nrel.gov/wind , *last viewed 8/24/07.*

[122] PhysOrg, "Full Speed Ahead: High-Temperature Conductors Ensure Efficient Propulsion in All-Electric Ships," April 11, 2007, PhysOrg, http://www.physorg.com/news95525363.html , *last viewed 8/24/07.*

[123] Engineer Live, "Silent Wind Turbine is Ultra-Efficient," Engineer Live, http://www.engineerlive.com/news/16981/silent-wind-turbine-is-ultraefficient.thtml , *last viewed 8/24/07.*

[124] ESRI, "ArcNews Online," ESRI, http://www.esri.com/news/arcnews/winter0607articles/minimizing-avian. html , *last viewed 8/24/07.*

[125] Lloyd Alter, "Mag-Wind Vertical Axis Turbine for Your Home," Treehugger, http://www.treehugger.com/files/2007/01/magwind_vertica.php , *last viewed 8/24/07.*

[126] US Department of Energy, Office of Energy Efficiency and Renewable Energy, "Report to Congress on Renewable Energy Resource Assessment Information for the United States," US Department of Energy, (October 2006), http://www.eere.energy.gov/ba/pba/km_portal/docs/pdf/fy06_epact_201_report.pdf , *last viewed 8/24/07.*

[127] Institute of Physics, "Did You Know?" http://www.einsteinyear.org/facts/physicsFacts , *last viewed 8/24/07.*

[128] Institute of Physics, "Did You Know?" http://www.einsteinyear.org/facts/physicsFacts , *last viewed*

8/24/07.

[129] FAO Agricultural Services Bulletins-128, "Renewable Biological Systems for Alternative Sustainable Energy Production," United Nations Food and Agriculture

Organization, Agriculture Department, http://www.fao.org/docrep/w7241e/w7241e05.htm#1.2.1%20 photosynthetic%20efficiency , *last viewed 8/24/07.*

[130] National Renewable Energy Laboratory, " NREL Newsroom," National Renewable Energy Laboratory, http://www.nrel.gov/news/discover/archives/07_january.html , *last viewed 8/24/07.*

[131] Ashley Seager, "How Mirrors Can Light Up The World," *The Guardian*, November 27, 2006, electronic edition, http://environment.guardian.co.uk/energy/story/0,1957908,00. html , *last viewed 8/24/07.*

[132] National Renewable Energy Laboratory, "Feature Stories," National Renewable Energy Laboratory, http://www.nrel.gov/features/07-06_deliver_clean.html , *last viewed 8/24/07*; but see, Peter Fairley, "Fixing the Power Grid," Technology Review, October 17, 2007, electronic edition, http://www.technologyreview.com/Energy/19584, *last viewed 10/31/07.*

[133] Ashley Seager, "How Mirrors Can Light Up The World," *The Guardian*, November 27, 2006, electronic edition, http://environment.guardian.co.uk/energy/story/0,1957908,00. html , *last viewed 8/24/07.*

[134] Monty Goodell, "Trigeneration," Trigeneration Technologies, http://www.cog1eneration.net/Trigeneration.htm , *last viewed*

8/24/07.

[135] US Department of Energy, Office of Energy Efficiency and Renewable Energy, "Report to Congress on Renewable Energy Resource Assessment Information for the United States," US Department of Energy, (October 2006), http://www.eere.energy.gov/ba/pba/km_portal/docs/pdf/fy06 _epact_201_report.pdf , *last viewed 8/24/07.*

[136] *Ibid.*

[137] *Ibid.*

[138] *Ibid.*

[139] Jessica Baker, "Energy From the Sea," *Technology Review,* July 1, 2006, electronic edition, http://www.technologyreview.com/Energy/17092 , *last viewed 8/24/07.*

[140] US Department of Energy, Office of Energy Efficiency and Renewable Energy, "Report to Congress on Renewable Energy Resource Assessment Information for the United States," US Department of Energy, (October 2006), http://www.eere.energy.gov/ba/pba/km_portal/docs/pdf/fy06 _epact_201_report.pdf , *last viewed 8/24/07.*

[141] US Department of Energy, Office of Energy Efficiency and Renewable Energy, "Report to Congress on Renewable Energy Resource Assessment Information for the United States," US Department of Energy, (October 2006),

http://www.eere.energy.gov/ba/pba/km_portal/docs/pdf/fy06 _epact_201_report.pdf , *last viewed 8/24/07.*

[142] State of Oregon, Department of Energy, "Biomass Energy," http://www.oregon.gov/ENERGY/RENEW/Biomass/BiomassHome.shtml , *last viewed 8/24/07.*

[143] Unisun Technologies, Ltd., "Biomass Energy," http://shimas-hosting.com/unisun/ biomass_energy.htm , *last viewed 8/24/07.*

[144] Plasco Energy Group, "News Releases," http://www.plascoenergygroup.com/content.php?cat=press&subcat=press90 , *last viewed 8/24/07.*

[145] U.S. Environmental Protection Agency, "Municipal Solid Waste in the United States: Facts and Figures," http://www.epa.gov/epaoswer/non-hw/muncpl/msw99.htm , *last viewed 8/24/07.*

[146] Energy Information Administration, "Electric Power Annual," U.S. Department of Energy, http://www.eia.doe.gov/cneaf/electricity/epa/epa_sum.html , *last viewed 8/24/07.*

[147] Michael Behar,"The Prophet of Garbage," Popular Science, March, 2007, electronic edition, http://www.popsci.com/popsci/science/873aae7bf86c0110vgnvcm1000004eecbccdrcrd.html , *last viewed 8/24/07.*

[148] Plasco Energy Group, "News Releases," http://www.plascoenergygroup.com/content.php?cat=press&subcat=press90 , *last viewed 8/24/07.*

[149] *USA Today*, "Florida County Plans to Vaporize Landfill," September 9, 2006, electronic edition, http://www.usatoday.com/news/nation/2006-09-09-fla-

countytrash_x.htm , *last viewed 8/24/07.*

[150] Plasco Energy Group,"AboutUs,"
http://www.plascoenergygroup.com/content.php?cat=about ,
last viewed 8/24/07.

[151] US Department of Energy, Office of Energy Efficiency and
Renewable Energy, "Alternative Fuels Data Center,"
http://www.eere.energy.gov/afdc/altfuel/ natural_gas.html , *last
viewed 8/24/07.*

[152] George Thomas and Jay Keller, "Hydrogen Storage-
Overview," Sandia National Laboratories,
<http://www1.eere.energy.gov/hydrogenandfuelcells/pdfs/bul
k_hydrogen_stor_pres_sandia.pdf, *last viewed 8/24/07.*

[153] Envestra, "About Natural Gas," <www.natural-
gas.com.au/about/reference.html, *last viewed 8/25/07.*

[154] George Thomas and Jay Keller, "Hydrogen Storage-
Overview," Sandia National Laboratories,
http://www1.eere.energy.gov/hydrogenandfuelcells/pdfs/bulk_
hydrogen_stor_pres_sandia.pdf, *last viewed 8/24/07.*

[155] Paul A. Kittle, "Alternate Daily Cover Materials and Subtitle
D- The Selection Technique," Rusmar Incorporated,
http://www.aquafoam.com/papers/selection.pdf, *last viewed
8/25/07.*

[156]George Thomas and Jay Keller, "Hydrogen Storage-
Overview," Sandia National Laboratories,
http://www1.eere.energy.gov/hydrogenandfuelcells/pdfs/bulk_
hydrogen_stor_pres_sandia.pdf, *last viewed 8/24/07.*

[157] Energy Information Administration, "Energy Calculator,"

U.S. Department of Energy,
www.eia.doe.gov/kids/energyfacts/science/energy_calculator.ht
ml, *last viewed 8/25/07.*

[158] UNH Biodiesel Group, "Alternative Fuel Vehicle
Comparison,"
www.unh.edu/p2/biodiesel/article_vehicle_compare.html, *last
viewed 8/25/07.*

[159] Kevin Bullis, "BP's Bet on Butanol," *Technology Review*, March
27, 2007, electronic edition,
http://www.technologyreview.com/Energy/18443/, *last viewed
8/25/07.*

[160] George Thomas and Jay Keller, "Hydrogen Storage-
Overview," Sandia National Laboratories,
http://www1.eere.energy.gov/hydrogenandfuelcells/pdfs/bulk_
hydrogen_stor_pres_sandia.pdf, *last viewed 8/24/07.*

[161] Lun Chen, "Energy in a Ton of Coal," The Physics Factbook,
http://hypertextbook.com/facts/2006/LunChen.shtml, *last
viewed 8/25/07.*

[162] No direct data on syngas energy density has been found. This
is based on statement found in Wikipedia that syngas contains
less than half the energy density of natural gas:
http://en.wikipedia.org/wiki/Syngas, *last viewed 8/25/07.*

[163] Jenny Hua, "Energy Density of Methanol (Wood Alcohol),"
The Physics Factbook,
http://hypertextbook.com/facts/2005/JennyHua.shtml, *last
viewed 8/25/07.*

[164] David E. Dirkse, "Some Energy Buffers,"
http://home.hccnet.nl/david.dirkse/math/energy.html, *last*

viewed 8/25/07.

[165] John Tanaka, "Batteries," The Energy Advocate, http://www.energyadvocate.com/batts.htm, last *viewed 8/25/07.*

[166] John Tanaka, "Batteries," The Energy Advocate, http://www.energyadvocate.com/batts.htm, last *viewed 8/25/07.*

[167] Science Daily, "Ethanol and Biodiesel From Crops Not Worth the Energy," July 6, 2005, www.sciencedaily.com/releases/2005/07/050705231841.htm, *last viewed 8/25/07.*

[168] The Energy Blog, "Butanol," James Fraser, http://thefraserdomain.typepad.com/energy/butanol/index.ht ml, *last viewed 8/25/07.*

[169] *Ibid.*

[170] PR Newswire, "DuPont and BP Announce Partnership to Develop Advanced Biofuels," June 20, 2006, electronic edition, http://www.prnewswire.com/mnr/dupont/24656, last viewed 8/25/07.

[171] U.S. Department of Agriculture, Economic Research Service, "Ethanol Reshapes the Corn Market," http://www.ers.usda.gov/AmberWaves/April06/Features/Etha nol.htm, *last viewed 8/25/07.*

[172] Science Daily, "New Success in Engineering Plant Oils," March 6, 2007 www.sciencedaily.com/releases/2007/03/070305202942.htm, *last viewed 8/26/07.*

[173] Journey to Forever, "Oil Yields and Characteristics," Keith

Addison, http://journeytoforever.org/biodiesel_yield.html, *last viewed 8/25/07.*

[174] *Ibid.*

[175] Science Daily, "Biofuel: Turning Old Fat into Jet Fuel," March 22, 2007
www.sciencedaily.com/releases/2007/03/070319175853.htm, *last viewed 8/25/07.*

[176] Kevin Bullis, "Algae-Based Fuels Set to Bloom," *Technology Review*, February 5, 2007, electronic edition,
http://www.technologyreview.com/ Energy/18138/, *last viewed 8/24/07.*

[177] John Sheehan *et al.*, "A Look Back at the U.S. Department of Energy's Aquatic Species Program: Biodiesel from Algae," U.S. Department of Energy, Office of Fuels Development,
http://www1.eere.energy.gov/biomass/pdfs/biodiesel_from_al gae.pdf, *last viewed 8/25/07.*

[178] Oligae, "Algal Biodiesel Characteristics and Properties," eSource India,
http://www.oilgae.com/algae/oil/biod/char/char.html, *last viewed 8/26/07.*

[179] GreenFuel Technologies Corporation, "Technology,"
www.greenfuelonline.com/technology.htm, *last viewed 8/25/07.*

[180] For instance: Dennis Normile, "Ceramic Captures CO_2," Design News, June 1, 2002,
http://www.designnews.com/article/CA219540.html, *last viewed 8/25/07.*

[181] Rakesh Agrawal *et al.*, "Sustainable Fuel for the

Transportation Sector," *Proceedings of the National Academy of Sciences*, March 14, 2007, electronic edition, http://dx.doi.org/10.1073/pnas.0609921104, *last viewed 8/25/07.*

[182] *Ibid.*

[183] U.S. Department of Energy, "Grid 2030," http://www.energetics.com/pdfs/electric_power/electric_visio n.pdf , last viewed 8/30/07.

[184] There is already evidence of convergence-divergence with the use of vehicle-to-grid technology which allows an automobile to power a household: Jim Motavalli, "Power to the People: Run Your House on a Prius," *The New York Times*, September 2, 2007, Automobiles p.5.

[185] David Talbot, "A More Robust Grid for Manhattan," *Technology Review*, May 29, 2007, electronic edition, www.technologyreview.com/Energy/18790, *last viewed 8/25/07.*

[186] Pekka E. Kaupi *et al.*, "Returning Forests Analyzed With the Forest Identity," *Proceedings of the National Academy of Sciences*, November 13, 2006, electronic edition, http://dx.doi.org/10.1073/pnas.0608343103, *last viewed 8/26/07.*

[187] This terminology is explained in the Introduction.

[188] Kirk Dombrowski, "The Praxis of Indigenism and Alaska Native Timber Politics," *American Anthropologist*, 2002, 104(4): 1062-1073; Mongabay, "Land Reform Agency Sanctions Logging in Amazon Rainforest Park," electronic edition, August 21, 2007, http://news.mongabay.com/2007/0821-amazon.html, *last viewed 9/1/07.*

[189] Edward B. Barbier, "Institutional Constraints and Deforestation: An Application to Mexico," *Economic Inquiry* (2002) 40:3, 508-519.

[190] The Gini Index is a measure of distributional equity. The higher the number, the lower the equity. This and other economic measures are fully explained in the Flawed Economics section of this volume.

[191] These Gini results are from the UN: NationMaster, "UN Gini Index," http://www.nationmaster.com/graph/eco_inc_equ_un_gin_ind -income-equality-un-gini-index, *last viewed 8/26/07*. According to more recent CIA data the Gini numbers are: Brazil = 60.7, Colombia = 57.1, CAR = 61.3, Guatemala = 55.8, Honduras = 56.3: CIA World Factbook, 2004, "Gini Index," http://www.umsl.edu/services/govdocs/wofact2004/fields/21 72.html, *last viewed 8/26/07*. The Congos, Gabon, Eq. Guinea, Suriname, and French Guyana are unreported by either agency.

[192] Ramón López, "Financing and Policy Mechanisms for Sustainable Use and Management of Forests," in *Forest Resource Policy in Latin America*, ed. K. Keipi, 39 (Baltimore, MD: Johns Hopkins University Press, 1998).

[193] William J. Broad, "Useful Mutants, Bred with Radiation," *The New York Times*, August 28, 2007, electronic edition, http://www.nytimes.com, *last viewed 8/28/07*.

[194] For coverage of GMO policies around the world see *Eutopia Monthly*: http://www.eutopianow.org, *last viewed 8/25/07*, and the *Eutopia Monthly* archive: http://www.xyvy.info, *last viewed 8/26/07*.

[195] Arpad Pustzai, "Genetically Modified Foods: Are They a Risk to Human/Animal Health?" ActionBioscience, http://actionbioscience.org/biotech/pusztai.html, *last viewed 9/2/07.*

[196] Union of Concerned Scientists, "Genetic Engineering," http://www.ucsusa.org/food_and_environment/genetic_engine ering, *last viewed 8/26/07.*

[197] Seedquest, "Global Status of Commercialized Biotech/GM Crops: 2006," January 18, 2007, http://www.seedquest.com/News/releases/2007/january/1814 5.htm, *last viewed 8/26/07.*

[198] Miguel A. Altieri, "The Ecological Impacts of Agricultural Technology," ActionBioscience, http://www.actionbioscience.org/biotech/altieri.html, *last viewed 8/26/07.*

[199] A. Vasemägi *et al.*, "Extensive Immigration from Compensatory Hatchery Releases into Wild Atlantic Salmon Population in the Baltic Sea: Spatio-Temporal Analysis Over 18 Years," *Heredity*, May 4, 2005, electronic edition, http://dx.doi.org/10.1038/sj.hdy.6800693, *last viewed 8/26/07.*

[200] GMWatch, "Andean Farmers Pick GM Potato Fight with Multinational Syngenta," January 16, 2007, http://www.gmwatch.org/archive2.asp?arcid=7464, *last viewed 8/26/07.*

[201] James D. Gaisford *et al.*, "Will the TRIPS Agreement Foster Appropriate Biotechnologies for Developing Countries?" *Journal of Agricultural Economics*, June 2007, electronic edition, http://dx.doi.org/10.1111/j.1477-9552.2007.00110.x, *last viewed*

8/26/07.

202 Dina Kraft, "From Far Beneath the Israeli Desert, Water Sustains a Fertile Enterprise," *The New York Times,* January 2, 2007, electronic edition, http://www.nytimes.com, *last viewed 1/02/07.*

203 Amy Feldman, "Skyscraper Farms," *Popular Science,* July 2007, electronic edition, http://www.popsci.com/popsci/environment/f2105a914b6b31 10vgnvcm1000004eecbccdrcrd.html, *last viewed 8/26/07.*

204 Michael Tennesen, "Black Gold of the Amazon," Discover, April 30, 2007, electronic edition, http://discovermagazine.com/2007/apr/black-gold-of-the-amazon, *last viewed 8/26/07.*

205 FDA Consumer Magazine, "Genetic Engineering: The Future of Foods?" U.S. Food and Drug Administration, November-December 2003, http://www.fda.gov/fdac/features/2003/603_food.html, *last viewed 8/26/07.*

206 Union of Concerned Scientists, "Genetic Engineering," http://www.ucsusa.org/food_and_environment/genetic_engine ering, *last viewed 8/26/07.*

207 Forest Stewardship Council, "Home Page," http://www.fsc.org/en, *last viewed 8/26/07.*

208 Sustainable Forestry Initiative, "Home Page," http://www.certifiedwoodsearch.org/sfiprogram, *last viewed 9/01/07.*

209 Programme for the Endorsement of Forest Certification

Schemes, "Home Page,"
www.pefc.org/internet/html/index.htm, *last viewed 8/27/07.*

[210] William McDonough and Michael Braungart, *Cradle to Cradle: Rethinking the Way We Make Things*, (New York: North Point Press, 2002.

[211] US Department of Energy, Office of Energy Efficiency and Renewable Energy, "Report to Congress on Renewable Energy Resource Assessment Information for the United States," US Department of Energy, (October 2006),
http://www.eere.energy.gov/ba/pba/km_portal/docs/pdf/fy06_epact_201_report.pdf, *last viewed 8/24/07.*

[212] Environmental Law Committee, "Incineration: Good or Bad for New York City?" Association of the Bar of the City of New York, March 22, 2007, podcast of debate,
http://www.nycbar.org/mp3/Incineration_discussion_32207.mp3, *last accessed 8/27/07.*

[213] SITA, Sita Mechanical Biological Treatment Position Paper,"
http://www.sita.co.uk/assets/PP_MBT.pdf, *last viewed 8/27/07.*

[214] *Ibid.*

[215] *Environmental News Service*, "Great Lakes Fouled by Raw Sewage," November 29, 2006, http://www.ens-newswire.com/ens/nov2006/2006-11-29-04.asp, *last viewed 8/27/07;* Daniel Pepper, "India's Rivers are Drowning in Pollution," CNN Money, June 4, 2007,
http://money.cnn.com/magazines/fortune/fortune_archive/2007/06/11/100083453/index.htm?postversion=2007060408, *last viewed 8/27/07;* BBC News, "Rain Forces Raw Sewage into River [Thames]," August 10, 2004, electronic edition,
http://news.bbc.co.uk/1/hi/england/london/3553052.stm, *last*

viewed 8/27/07.

[216] UNESCO, "2nd UN World Water Development Report, 2006,"
http://www.unesco.org/water/wwap/wwdr2/table_contents.sh
tml, *last viewed 8/28/07.*

[217] Kris Christen, "Removing Nutrients and Pharmaceuticals,"
Environmental Science and Technology, online edition, (2007) 41(3):
672-673,
http://pubs.acs.org/subscribe/journals/esthag/41/i03/html/02
0107news5.html, *last viewed 8/27/07.*

[218] U.S. Environmental Protection Agency, "How Wastewater
Treatment Works...the Basics,"
http://www.epa.gov/npdes/pubs/bastre.pdf, *last viewed
8/27/07.*

[219] U.S. Environmental Protection Agency, "Municipal
Technologies," http://www.epa.gov/owmitnet/mtb/index.htm,
last viewed 8/27/07.

[220] Wang, Li-Sha *et al.*, "Effect of Ammonia Nitrogen and
Dissolved Organic Matter Fractions on the Genotoxicity of
Wastewater Effluent during Chlorine Disinfection,"
Environmental Science and Technology, online edition, (2007) 41(1):
160-165, http:dx.doi.org/ 10.1021/es0616635, *last viewed
8/27/07.*

[221] PhysOrg, "What's in the Water? Estrogenic Activity
Documented in Fish Caught in Pittsburgh's Rivers,"
http://www.physorg.com/news96035578.html, *last viewed
8/31/07.*

[222] Kris Christen, "Removing Nutrients and Pharmaceuticals,"

Environmental Science and Technology, online edition, (2007) 41(3): 672-673,
http://pubs.acs.org/subscribe/journals/esthag/41/i03/html/02
0107news5.html, *last viewed 8/27/07*.

223 Niina M. Vieno *et al.*, "Occurrence of Pharmaceuticals in River Water and Their Elimination in a Pilot-Scale Drinking Water Treatment Plant," *Environmental Science and Technology*, June 15, 2007, electronic edition, 41(14): 5077-5084, http://dx.doi.org/ 10.1021/es062720x, *last viewed 8/27/07*.

224 The News Tribune, "Drugs Found in Oregon Streams," electronic edition,
http://www.thenewstribune.com/359/story/57194.html, *last viewed 8/27/07*.

225 Science Daily, "New Sustainable Plant Source of Omega 3," March 31, 2007,
http://www.sciencedaily.com/releases/2007/03/070330231448.
htm, *last viewed 8/27/07*.

226 United States Patent 5476975, "Extraction of Toxic Organic Contaminants from Wood and Photodegradation of Toxic Organic Contaminants," *FreePatentsOnline*,
http://www.freepatentsonline.com/5476975.html, *last viewed 8/27/07;* Mura, G.M. *et al.*, "Photodegradation of Organic Waste Coupling Hydrogenase and Titanium Dioxide," *Annals of the New York Academy of Sciences*, 879: 267-75,
http://dx.doi.org/10.1111/j.1749-6632.1999.tb10430.x, last viewed 8/27/07; Tanizaki, Teiji *et al.*, "Photodegradation of Organic Compounds in Tap Water using High Reactive Titanium Dioxide," *Journal of Environmental Chemistry*, 2005 15(4): 847-853, http://sciencelinks.jp/j-
east/article/200602/000020060206A0010017.php, *last viewed 8/27/07*.

[227] See for example: Chicago Climate Exchange, "Home Page," http://www.chicagoclimatex.com/index.jsf, *last viewed 9/2/07.*

[228] *USA Today*, "Florida County Plans to Vaporize Landfill," September 9, 2006, electronic edition, http://www.usatoday.com/news/nation/2006-09-09-fla-county-trash_x.htm, *last viewed 8/24/07.*

[229] MIT Interdisciplinary Panel, "The Future of Nuclear Power," 2003, http://web.mit.edu/nuclearpower, *last viewed 8/23/07.*

[230] The Global Programme of Action for the Protection of the Marine Environment from Land-Based Activities, "Home Page," United Nations Environmental Programme, www.gpa.unep.org, *last viewed 8/29/07.*

[231] Environmental Facilities Fund, "Clean Water State Revolving Fund (CWSRF)," New York State, http://www.nysefc.org/home/index.asp?page=14, *last viewed 8/28/07.*

[232] Clean Water America, "Funding At Risk," http://www.cleanwateramerica.org/theissue/index.cfm?ID=8, *last viewed 8/28/07.*

[233] *Ibid.*

[234] U.S. Geological Survey, "Eutrophication," http://toxics.usgs.gov/definitions/eutrophication.html, *last viewed 8/28/07.*

[235] United Nations Environment Programme, "Further Rise in Number of Marine 'Dead Zones'," http://www.unep.org/Documents.Multilingual/Default.asp?Arti

cleID=5393&DocumentID=486&l=en, *last viewed 8/28/07*.

[236] Public Broadcasting Service, "Crown of Thorns, Wetlands Nitrogen,"
http://www.pbs.org/strangedays/episodes/troubledwaters/experts/deadzones.html, *last viewed 8/28/07*.

[237]

[238] Kris Christen, "Rewarding Fertilizer Pollution with Crop Subsidies," *Environmental Science and Technology*, http://pubs.acs.org/subscribe/journals/esthag-w/2007/june/science/kc_nitrate.html, *last viewed 8/29/07*.

[239] Michael Tennesen, "Black Gold of the Amazon," Discover, April 30, 2007, electronic edition, http://discovermagazine.com/2007/apr/black-gold-of-the-amazon, *last viewed 8/26/07*.

[239] Forest Stewardship Council, "Home Page," www.fsc.org/en, *last viewed 8/29/07*.

[240] Dina Kraft, "From Far Beneath the Israeli Desert, Water Sustains a Fertile Enterprise," *The New York Times*, January 2, 2007, electronic edition, http://www.nytimes.com, *last viewed 1/02/07*.

[241] Food and Agriculture Organization of the United Nations (FAO), "Fishery Statistics Programme," http://www.fao.org/fi/statist/statist.asp, last viewed 8/28/07.

[242] Food and Agriculture Organization of the United Nations (FAO), "The State of World Fisheries and Aquaculture 2006," http://www.fao.org/docrep/009/A0699e/A0699e00.htm, *last viewed 8/28/07*.

[243] Food and Agriculture Organization of the United Nations (FAO), "Fishery Statistics Programme," http://www.fao.org/fi/statist/statist.asp, last viewed 8/28/07.

[244] D. Pauly *et al.*, "Down With Fisheries, Up With Aquaculture: Implications of Global Trends in the Mean Trophic Levels of Fishes," Paper presented at meeting of the American Association for the Advancement of Science, 15–20 February 2001, San Francisco, California.

[245] Rebecca J. Goldburg, *et al.*, "Marine Aquaculture in the United States: Environmental Impacts and Policy Options," Pew Oceans Commission, http://www.pewtrusts.org/pdf/env_pew_oceans_aquaculture.pdf, *last viewed 8/28/07.*

[246] Barry Costa-Pierce and Alan Desbonnet, "A Future Urban Ecosystem Incorporating Urban Aquaculture for Wastewater Treatment and Food Production," in *Urban Aquaculture*, ed. Barry Costa-Pierce (Wallingford, Oxfordshire, UK: CAB International, 2005).

[247] *Ibid.*

[248] For coverage of aquaculture science research from around the world see *Eutopia Monthly*: http://www.eutopianow.org, *last viewed 8/25/07*, and the *Eutopia Monthly* archive: http://www.xyvy.info, *last viewed 8/26/07.*

[249] Kare C. Seto and Michael Fragkias, "Mangrove Conversion and Aquaculture Development in Vietnam: A Remote Sensing-Based Approach for Evaluating the Ramsar Convention on Wetlands," *Global Environmental Change*, electronic edition, http://dx.doi.org/10.1016/j.gloenvcha.2007.03.001, *last viewed*

8/28/07.

[250] Snapperfarm, "Home Page," http://www.snapperfarm.com, *last viewed 8/28/07.*

[251] Robin McKie, "Water Power Puts Climate in Peril," Guardian Unlimited: The Observer, electronic edition, December 3, 2006, http://www.guardian.co.uk/science/2006/dec/03/globalwarmi ng.energy, *last viewed 8/27/07.*

[252] Science Daily, "Going Nowhere Fast: Top Rivers Face Mounting Threats," http://www.sciencedaily.com/releases/2007/03/070320201948. htm, *last viewed 8/28/07.*

[253] For coverage of environmental conditions affecting lakes around the world see *Eutopia Monthly*: http://www.eutopianow.org, *last viewed 8/25/07*, and the *Eutopia Monthly* archive: http://www.xyvy.info, *last viewed 8/26/07.*

[254] Rhett A. Butler, "Mangroves More Threatened Than Rainforests," *Mongabay*, http://news.mongabay.com/2007/0705-mangroves.html, *last viewed 8/28/07.*

[255] United Nations Environment Programme, "Further Rise in Number of Marine 'Dead Zones'," http://www.unep.org/Documents.Multilingual/Default.asp?Arti cleID=5393&DocumentID=486&l=en, *last viewed 8/28/07.*

[256] Clive Wilkinson, ed., "Status of Coral Reefs of the World: 2004," Australian Institute of Marine Science, http://www.aims.gov.au/pages/research/coral-bleaching/scr2004/index.html, *last viewed 8/28/07.*

[257] United Nations Environmental Programme, "Groundwater

and its Susceptibility to Degradation: A Global Assessment of the Problem and Options for Management," http://www.unep.org/DEWA/water/groundwater/groundwater_report.asp, *last viewed 8/29/07.*

[258] U.S. Environmental Protection Agency, "Water Quality Trading," http://www.epa.gov/owow/watershed/trading.htm, *last viewed 8/28/07.*

[259] Innovations Report, "Tradable Biodiversity Rights Can Help Conserve Species Richness," March 2, 2007, www.innovations-report.de/html/berichte/umwelt_naturschutz/bericht-79965.html, *last viewed 8/28/07.*

[260] Rainforest Alliance, "Sustainable Agriculture," http://www.rainforest-alliance.org/programs/agriculture, *last viewed 11/03/07.*

[261] World Bank, "Shaping the Future of Water for Agriculture," 2005, http://siteresources.worldbank.org/INTARD/Resources/Shaping_the_Future_of_Water_for_Agriculture.pdf, *last viewed 8/29/07.*

[262] Global Environmental Facility, "GEF Funding," http://www.gefweb.org/interior.aspx?id=44, *last viewed 8/29/07.*

[263] World Bank, "World Bank Lending by Theme and Sector," http://web.worldbank.org/WBSITE/EXTERNAL/EXTABOUTUS/EXTANNREP/EXTANNREP2K6/0,,contentMDK:21047181~pagePK:64168445~piPK:64168309~theSitePK:2838572,00.html , *last viewed 8/29/07.*

[264] National Campaign for Sustainable Agriculture, "Home Page," http://www.sustainableagriculture.net, *last viewed*

8/29/07.

[265] International Rivers Network, "Home Page," http://www.irn.org, *last viewed 8/29/07.*

[266] The Nature Conservancy, "Home Page," http://www.nature.org/?src=t1, *last viewed 8/29/07.*

[267] Robert Howarth, "Bringing Coastal Dead Zones Back to Life," ActionBioscience, http://www.actionbioscience.org/environment/howarth.html, *last viewed 9/2/07.*

[268] John Seabrook, "Sowing for the Apocalypse," *The New Yorker,* August 27, 2007, 60-71.

[269] Robert M. Solow, "Sustainability: An Economist's Perspective," in *Economics of the Environment 4th Edition,* ed. Robert N. Stavins (New York: W.W. Norton & Co., 2000).

[270] Corrado Gini, "Measurement of Inequality and Incomes," *The Economic Journal,* 1921, 31: 124-126.

[271] These figures come from the United Nations and are somewhat dated being from the year 2000: NationMaster, "UN Gini Index," http://www.nationmaster.com/graph/eco_inc_equ_un_gin_ind -income-equality-un-gini-index, *last viewed 8/26/07.* The CIA also publishes these numbers with somewhat more recent data: Central Intelligence Agency, "The World Factbook: Gini Index," https://www.cia.gov/library/publications/the-world-factbook/fields/2172.html, *last viewed 8/29/07.* For the sake of consistency I used only the UN data for this report. According to the CIA, the only differences from the UN figures for this list of countries are: US = 45, China = 44, Chile = 53.8.

[272] United Nations Statistics Division, "Millenium Indicators Database," http://mdgs.un.org, *last viewed 8/29/07.*

[273] It is important to remember that population growth statistics often include not only birth and death information but immigration versus emigration numbers as well. A country showing a high rate of population growth may be receiving many immigrants and thus be alleviating natural population pressures from another country. A low population growth rate could actually be cloaking a large natural rate with heavy numbers of emigrants.

[274] Partha Dasgupta, "The Population Problem: Theory and Evidence," *Journal of Economic Literature*, December 1995, Vol. 33, 1879-1902.

[275] The CIA's more recent data indicates that the US Gini is at 45, which is indicative of movement away from equitable distribution in recent years.

[276] The CIA Gini for Russia is 40.5.

[277] See: Branko Milanovic, "Worlds Apart: Measuring International and Global Inequality," Princeton University Press, http://press.princeton.edu/titles/7946.html, *last viewed 8/29/07.*

[278] U.N. Atlas of Global Inequality, "Home Page," University of California at Santa Cruz, http://ucatlas.ucsc.edu, *last viewed 8/29/07.*

[279] Nationmaster, " Donor Per Capita by Country," www.nationmaster.com/graph/eco_eco_aid_don_percap-economic-aid-donor-per-capita, *last viewed 8/29/07.*

[280] For evaluations of many charitable organizations, see *Charity Navigator* at http://charitynavigator.org/index.cfm?bay=content.view&cpid =628, *last viewed 8/29/07*.

[281] See for instance: PropertyRights.org, http://propertyrights.org, *last viewed 8/30/07*, or Property Rights Foundation of America, http://prfamerica.org, *last viewed 8/30/07*.

[282] Robert Repetto *et al.*, "Has Environmental Protection Really Reduced Productivity Growth?" *Challenge*, January-February 1997, 46-57; Michael E. Porter and Claas van der Linde, "Toward a New Conception of the Environment-Competitiveness Relationship," *Journal of Economic Perspectives*, 1995 9(4): 97-118.

[283] Karen Palmer *et al.*, "Tightening Environmental Standards: The Benefit-Cost or the No-Cost Paradigm?" *Journal of Economic Perspectives*, 1995 9(4): 119-132.

[284] *Ibid.*

[285] Adam B. Jaffe and Steven R. Peterson, "Environmental Regulation and the Competitiveness of U.S. Manufacturing," *Journal of Economic Literature*, 1995, 33: 132-163.

[286] World Trade Organization, "Sanitary and Phytosanitary Measures Agreement," http://www.wto.org/english/docs_e/legal_e/15-sps.pdf, *last viewed 8/30/07;* World Trade Organization, "Technical Barriers to Trade Agreement," http://www.wto.org/english/docs_e/legal_e/17-tbt.pdf, *last viewed 8/30/07*.

287 Robert M. Solow, "Sustainability: An Economist's Perspective," in *Economics of the Environment 4th Edition*, ed. Robert N. Stavins (New York: W.W. Norton & Co., 2000).

288 The Nature Conservancy, "Conservancy Purchases Federal Trawling Permits and Vessels to Protect Marine Areas in California," http://www.nature.org/wherewework/northamerica/states/california/press/trawlers062706.html, *last viewed 8/30/07.*

289 See: William McDonough and Michael Braungart, *Cradle to Cradle: Rethinking the Way We Make Things*, (New York: North Point Press, 2002.

290 See: Paul Hawken, Amory Lovins, and L. Hunter Lovins, *Natural Capitalism: Creating the Next Industrial Revolution*, online edition, http://www.natcap.org/sitepages/pid5.php, *last viewed 8/31/07.*

291 Herman Daly, *Beyond Growth: The Economics of Sustainable Development*, (Boston: Beacon Press, 1997).

292 United Nations Population Information Network, "Home Page," http://www.un.org/popin, *last viewed 8/30/07.*

293 U.S. Environmental Protection Agency, "Green Power Partnership: Partner List," http://www.epa.gov/greenpower/partners/gpp_partners.htm, *last viewed 8/30/07.*

294 Eco-Labels, "The Consumer Union's Guide to Eco Labels," http://www.eco-labels.org, *last viewed 8/30/07.*

295 Erwin Schrödinger, *What Is Life?*, (New York: Macmillan,

1946).

[296] Nicholas Georgescu-Roegen, *The Entropy Law and the Economic Process*, (Lincoln, Nebraska: iUniverse, 1999).

[297] Sometimes referred to as Syntropy, this concept is developed in the works of Léon Brillouin, *Science and Information Theory*, (New York: Dover Press, 2004), Luigi Fantappiè, *Opere Scelte*, (Bologna: Unione Matematica Italiana, 1973), and Albert Szent-Györgyi, "Drive in Living Matter to Perfect Itself," *Synthesis 1*, 1(1): 14-26, among others. One of the most readable articulations of these concepts may be found in Herman Daly's *Beyond Growth: The Economics of Sustainable Development*, (Boston: Beacon Press, 1997).

[298] *American Heritage Dictionary of the English Language, Fourth Edition*, "Entropy," (New York: Houghton Mifflin, 2007).

[299] Rudolf Clausius, "On Several Convenient Forms of the Fundamental Equations of the Mechanical Theory of Heat," *Annalen der Physik und Chemie*, (1850) 79: 368-397, 500-524.

[300] *McGraw-Hill Encyclopedia of Science and Technology*, "Entropy," (New York: McGraw-Hill, 2005).

[301] *American Heritage Dictionary of the English Language, Fourth Edition*, "Entropy," (New York: Houghton Mifflin, 2007).

[302] Erwin Schrödinger, *What Is Life?*, (New York: Macmillan, 1946).

[303] Some of the actions that I have taken: I am supporting three children in the developing world, I have lowered my energy consumption and purchased enough renewable energy credits to become carbon negative, I have brought my ecological footprint

to the 7.5 to 9.3 global acres range which means I am a producing an ecological surplus, I give an annual 3% of my income to reputable environmental or poverty reduction organizations, use solar power for many of my electronics, I regularly urge my political representatives to vote for effective environmental legislation, and have made enormous and numerous lifestyle changes in accord with Negentropy.

[304] *American Heritage Dictionary of the English Language, Fourth Edition*, "Hysteresis," (New York: Houghton Mifflin, 2007).

[305] British Antarctic Survey, "Antarctic Zone," http://www.antarctica.ac.uk/met/jds/ozone/index.html#bulletins, *last viewed 8/31/07.*